A DEBT PAID IN INK: THE SALVATION OF SANITY IN THREE ACTS

FROM THE HEART, MIND, AND SOUL OF:

CLYDE HURLSTON

copyright © 2020. Second edition by Clyde Hurlston. All rights reserved. Printed in the United States Of America. This book may not be reproduced or reprinted without prior approval from the author unless otherwise stated. Thank you for your purchase.

www.clydehurlston.com

facebook.com/adebtpaidinink
@adebtpaidinink

book design: Mitch Green

A DEBT PAID IN INK

ACT I
THE JOYS OF MARTYRDOM

Apple Of My Eye

Since that day in the garden, women have been blamed for the downfall of men. Whether it was Lilith or her replacement, Eve. Or let's not forget the cursed like Pandora or Cassandra. Throughout time, the fairer have been blamed for all of the ills of this world.

But what of her then?
This forbidden apple of my eye?

Am I to be cursed with expulsion if I were to succumb to her touch? Would I know the fires of damnation, for becoming acquainted with her taste? Well, take this truth as a confession, for I do not care. Whether her halo hides horns, it matters not. She is an angel that has saved me from the hell within myself.

And if that earns my place amongst the fallen, then I bid them to make room within the flames. Because my list of regrets shall never know her name. But these four walls will hear her call mine. Not in vain, but from the most delightful sort of pain.

Famished

There is a thought consuming me in this moment.
Gnawing at my eyes as if it is dying for attention.
And like always, it is her. The way she lies upon the bed.
Ever motionless, but so alive. Her hip rising from the
sheets, like the hills in Wicklow.

And I am silent.
Dying to journey into the valley hidden by the satin.
I so badly want a taste. But how do you wake an angel
when she sleeps? Is there a polite way to say, "I hunger
for you and dreams only leave me famished?"
But no, there's not. And so, I taste her like there's
no tomorrow. And judging from her hands in my hair,
along with that breathtaking arch in her back...
I don't think she minds.

At The Mercy Of A Gift

Seems I'm damned if I do and if I don't, but my resolve's remaining strong. I could apologize but I won't, It's not my fault I get taken wrong. I just bleed my ink unto a page, hoping to relieve my pain. Some may revere me as a sage, but on days like this it's all in vain. 'Cause the feeling comes and then it goes, what I will write, nobody knows. I'm at the mercy of a gift, and I never knew I'd cause a rift. Between myself and those who read, my every line and seem to need. Loyalty in subjects chose, no matter if it's rhyme or prose. Now I fight the urge to bite my tongue, 'cause I hear it hurts too much. And my mouth isn't fond of blood, so I won't allow my teeth to touch. For I'd rather speak with open mind, or merely write with sharp intent. But I sometimes have to find, just where my inspiration went. 'Cause the feeling comes and then it goes, what I will write nobody knows. I'm at the mercy of a gift, and I never knew I'd cause a rift. Between myself and those who read, my every line and seem to need. Loyalty in subjects chose, no matter if it's rhyme or prose. So what would you have me do, as I sit with pen in hand? Should I paint my point of view, and hope you'll understand? Or should I sit in fear, thinking you won't like the way? I chose to make you hear, the things I'd like to say. 'Cause I'd rather feel your hatred, for expressing what's within. Than to sit and leave you bored, In the quiet's grip again.

So please make up your mind, if you'd like to censor me.
But you better not complain, when you don't get a
sense of me. 'Cause you'll have no one else to blame,
when you can't figure out. The depths of how I feel,
or the heights I'm all about. 'Cause then you'll be mad
at me, and I'll come off that pedestal. Pulled down
by gravity, and that card you chose to pull. From
underneath your sleeve, to rest upon the face. Of this
tired table here, upon which I will rest my case.
'Cause the feeling comes, and then it goes. What I
will write, nobody knows. I'm at the mercy of a gift,
and I never knew I'd cause a rift. Between myself
and those who read. My every line, and seem to need.
Loyalty in subjects chose, no matter if it's rhyme or
prose. And I'll continue making lines rhyme at the end,
but there's a reason for it, my friend. Call the thing a
need if you must, but it's a compulsion I can trust.
To not destroy my life and exercise each shred of
strife. Until the pain is all but gone. I'll fill the page,
and carry on. And say fuck their little need to criticize
my rhyme or prose, 'cause they deserve the thorns
If they want to look past the rose...

Greet Me With A Smile

Oh, magnetic mistress, won't you miss me with your ways? 'Cause I've been down upon my knees, for what's feeling close to days. But looking deep inside your eyes, I know you'll just prolong my pain. While taking pleasure in the fact, I'm bold enough to now complain. But you've been on the shorter end, Of Charlie's little stick. Too many men have walked on you, and left you feeling sick. So now you'll take it out on me, and I'll enjoy it for awhile. 'Cause I'll spill every tear my dear, If you will greet me with a smile. Oh, magnetic mistress, Won't you miss me with your flame? 'Cause though I am a lowly moth, I'm losing patience for the game. That you've been steady playing here, while shining light upon my shame. 'Cause when your friends are not around, we both know you'll scream my name. So come, magnetic mistress, won't you tell me why you cry? Is it because those other fools, chose to leave the well this dry? See? You've been so busy burning me, you've overlooked some things. Like when your love is pouring down, you'll feel the joy it brings. But you'll have to loosen up my chains, and then undo a little rope. If I'm to get you on your back, and breathe the life into your hope...

Prism

I find myself stumbling through memories. Recalling every goddess that got away. But in retrospect, it was for the best...Maybe for them, I was just a prism. Bending light around my hopes, as to illuminate the things that they were supposed to find. Those things that I seemingly didn't possess. And in all honesty, I did have some soul-searching to do. I had grown too comfortable, using past hurts and disappointments as bricks and mortar. Building walls to hide from the world. Challenging those who thought themselves worthy, to climb and get me. But who has time for that shit? Too long I have accused others of putting me on a cross, to die for the sins of others. Not realizing that, in my state of apathy, I have done the exact, same thing to them.

Stock & Trade

Tell me your deepest, darkest desire. Tell me of things that warm you there, even on the coldest of nights. Tell me the thoughts you fear would bring you judgment. Take the shackles off your heart, and whisper to me your wishes. I would grant them for you. Just the two of us alone. No one else would ever know. Secrets are my stock and trade, darling. Your pleasure, my only currency.

The only thing that matters to me. I will give you this with no strings attached. No soul to trade, no paradise to be cast down from. You can resume your place in the picture perfect frame. Word of warning though...

I'm told I can be addictive to some. So keep that thought, in the mind I wish to help you lose.

CLYDE HURLSTON

Roses & Vines

I am not a rose, darling. I am a vine.
I will never impress you with my first,
stricken pose. But rather, you will
come to find, I've grown on you in
time. So while others may blossom
and bloom, and remove the air, from
a bustling room. I will not. I will, however,
twist and turn, and reach and yearn;
until a place within your grace,
is what I've earned. This hope, is all
I've got. So please do not rip me away from
you, Before I've had my chance to
stretch. Because, if given a fair amount
of nights and days, I may be the
greatest thing, your garden is ever
going to catch.

That is, if you'll have me.
And darling, you can.
You can have me any way you
want me. Just shhh, don't tell
the world…

Promethean Fire

The ancients lived their lives by the stars. They moved Heaven and Earth, Creating kingdoms for generations. Pyramids were erected. Monoliths were raised, And other wonders left behind. Signals made to their gods, Humbly drawn with Nazca lines.
But here in the present day, we are lost in translation. Still ignorant to the hidden knowledge. Much too vain for the arcane. Yet, I am an alchemist at heart. Hoping to transmute this ink into gold. Making each phrase a beacon, to lead her back to me. Dying to speak to the ancient within her, And truly earn her worship. Using the only thing I have left: The Promethean fire within my soul. The place where I forge these words.

CLYDE HURLSTON

These Are But Thoughts

These are but thoughts, gnawing at my mind. Sightly piercing through my days. And tunneling through my nights. Ideas more contagious than a virus. And visions more revered than a portrait. It is a want and a need, simultaneously. To be simply, greater than I am. It takes some courage to say aloud. For you first must acknowledge imperfections. And be more intimate with your flaws than your qualities. Because you know that when things can be improved, a day's work is never done. And then, sadly, life is no longer infinite. The days are not long enough. And the nights are far too dark to see through. But when the sun bleeds into the blue, and seeps its' way into your eyes, you know then, that another opportunity to improve shines before you. Glowing like a true virgin, on her wedding night. Or a Messiah's afternoon walk on the surface of a lake. The impossible can be made into flesh. And for all my thinking, for all my rambling, I am a coward. Too afraid to step forward. Too timid to endure the pain. The pain that comes from weakness leaving the body. For progress is birthed only by sacrifice. Greatness can only be reached by shedding mediocrity. And doubt is the slippery slope upon which one can find stagnation. But to escape this downward free fall, one must slay doubt. One must use the fire that is feeling fearless, to forge one's will into steel. Reflecting a tiger's eyes, and sharp as Excalibur of lore. Jumping high into the blue, and plunging this metaphoric weapon, into the negative thoughts plaguing your determination. This is what I must do. This is what we all must do. For all of the talk of how this world will end. For each fatalistic religion hoping to show the world their book was right. It feels like I am running out of time. Like the bottom of the hourglass is getting as heavy as I have been, for most of my young life. But as I've said before, these are but thoughts. Gnawing at my mind. Sightly piercing through my days. And tunneling through my nights. And after years of showing the world my faults. And having them be witness to my falls. Maybe, just maybe it's time. For more than my imagination to start taking flight. But is it too late for me?

And I Have? Nothing.

It seems that in the past, all great artists and minds, have shared similarities. Most were innovators in their time. And souls off which, imitators made their dime. Some were revered for their creations, by the public. Some were reviled for their creations, by institutions. But one glaring similarity I have noticed, is that many have had a muse. Dante had his Beatrice. And Yeats, he had his Maud. Manet had Victorine. While Francoise was Picasso's gift from God. Rodin had his Camile. Nietzsche and Freud shared a Lou. While Elena captivated Dali, and a great many others too. But what about me? One so alive in this hell. My friend, i have nothing. But this great tale to tell. And you could try to say, that it won't stay this way. But something has to burn, for inspiration to return... And even in the world of fiction, others have had their muse as well. Poor Eric Draven lost his Shelly, so he returned from dead. Ariadne aided Theseus, with both a sword and ball of thread. Then there was the tired soul who had lost his dear Lenore. He cried until a raven came and had squawked its', "nevermore." But what about me? One so alive in this hell. My friend, i have nothing. But this great tale to tell. And you could try to say, that it won't stay this way. But something has to burn, for inspiration to return...

But once I had willing muse, who threw her hat into the ring. But she revealed herself a widow black, and her bite it left a sting. But alas, i saw the venom fade and we became greater friends in time. Now she has another in her web, and her attention is no longer mine.

And that is truly fitting in a way, because her happiness was found. But now I sit with Lady Luck, driving my soul into the ground. While Mother Nature does her best, to make my city's river swell. Will I drown or spend my life alone? That's what I cannot seem to tell. 'Cause old Father Time's been unkind, since it's confidence i lack. And so now my heavy heart of stone, has begun to show a crack. So let me burn the waiting bridge, before a goddess tries to cross. My inner sea of misery, and then finds her life is at a loss. For the way I see the world would erode everything. That made her who she was, or made her want to sing. And she's far too beautiful, to deserve such a fate. So maybe it's for the best, that this wretch will have to wait. And say, so what about me? One so alive in this hell. My friend, i have nothing. But this great tale to tell. And this trail of ink should prove, that i have burned for long. Long enough to want to move, and have some darling prove him wrong. But this inner sea he mentioned, has now overtaken land. So now all this writer wants, is for his public to understand.

Amongst The Butterflies

I used to stroke your wings, but I didn't like the feel. 'Cause all the scrapes and minor cuts, would never seem to heal. And the wounds would surely sit, displayed and poorly dressed. While your smile would shine, and sins were not confessed. But your truths shall seek the light, though darkness suits them best. And two wrongs won't make a right, but they'll help to put my soul at rest. 'Cause you used to fan the flames, that raged inside of us. But once we got past your games, all that's left was lust. So now the wounds will surely sit, for all the world to see. And your fraud has now exposed, just how cloudy pearls can be. 'Cause your truths shall seek the light, though darkness suits them best. And two wrongs won't make a right, but they'll help to put my soul at rest. For I know I have my faults, and mistakes surely know my name. But I don't go around pretending that I'm impervious to blame. And I understand a butterfly's allure, fuels your need for being one. But my friend, I recognize a fellow moth, every time I'm seeing one. So now your truths shall seek the light, though darkness suits them best. and two wrongs won't make a right, but they'll help to put my soul at rest. 'Cause after all, what's a moth without the flame?

Icarus Of Lore

Once inside a sky so blue, I flew too high and fell to you. Reaching high I burned each wing, while placing blame on everything. And everyone that lies in sight, as if my rage will make it right. And Father warned his foolish youth, but I ignored his words of truth. So my fall was fast and swift, the waiting sea destroyed each feathered gift. And as the wax began to run, I felt my faith become undone. So I screamed into the skies, and yet he never once replied. So I'll never know the sweet caress, of the one who'll put my soul at rest. Oh, I had to rise before the fall, just to prove I'll never know it all, but I've longed to feel this free, and then you took the world from me. Still I rose and rose some more, just like Icarus of lore. But then I came crashing down, and saw that you were not around. So now I fall and fall again, hoping you would let me in. But when I'm crashing down this fast, I'm easier to just look past. Won't you catch me, catch me, if you can? Oh what say you, Son Of Man? Have I never earned the right to fly? Oh, must our passions be the reason that we die?

By My Actions, Am I Bound

I am chained to a rock on a nameless cliff; at the outer edge of the world, and I await. Patiently, I wait. On a violation ordered by a God, that will come swooping down from the sky he sits upon. For my better parts to be plundered now, by a winged beast with righteous beak. And yet, at night my parts will return pristine. So they'll be consumed when morrow comes. But what would cause such a ghastly sight, is probably what your lips would ask. And whether you feel it's wrong or right, this punishment is for a task. That I once chose to embark upon, by giving a gift of warmth to lowly man. And by the time the day was gone, I knew that my consequence was now at hand. For fate could not be tempted friend, without the scales falling out of place. And by placing weight on either end, it was like a slap across a godly face. So from Olympus Mount came a verdict loud, that would last throughout eternity. And while I stood among the foolish proud, I can now feel humility return to me. For I'm certain I can win no pity, and that these troubles are my own. And if some soul would come to get me, they would endure a hell alone. So they would be better off advised, to just let this eagle feed. For his will won't be compromised, and I don't foresee getting the mercy I may need. So it is by my actions that I am bound, to this rock that never rolls. And as I am devoured upon this ground, know that I don't regret my molding of the souls. Who will never know the burdens borne, by the ones so close to gods. And in closing, I was a fool to just ignore, his wrath and play the odds...

A DEBT PAID IN INK

For The Ones Who Read

As reality seeped into her dreams, relationships mirror fantasies on the screen. Flickering just in front her bed, having influence on what occurs inside her head. She wakes slowly as if trying to fight, the early ending of a blissful night. But alas, her struggle is all for naught, she can't regain that in which she sought. Tired from a day's worth of time, running mazes deep inside her mind. Wondering if she will ever find a man, one who will finally try to understand. The things with her that go unsaid, spoken in little signs that often go unread. With technology's non-stop advance, she wonders if she will ever have the chance. To catch the one in her world wide web, and make her impression stick to him instead. Her past attempts ended all the same, wondering if it is herself that she must blame. With food for thought, she wished to feed them. With a pen, she wrote her dreams across her breasts, in hopes that a man will finally read them. Because she displays herself like an open book, but they only offer her a fleeting look. For they judge books like her solely by their covers, and she often made the illiterate her only lovers. And the things that never made sense to me, was how she would show them the book's contents for free. So how would they appreciate the words, when they could easily touch the pages that were hers? But to me, this book is indeed a masterpiece, and I would read every word if the abuse would cease. But in this world, with pleasure just a click away, do we value anything that will actually stay? On a shelf or desk, to finally gather dust. But to me it seems the world would rather lust. To be gratified instantly, to make them feel fulfilled, and foolishly ignore every drop of sweat we've ever spilled. Like those drops were written on our face, and we were sculptures tightly held in place. For the amusement of those who don't appreciate the art, or those hoping time would help us fall apart. But our souls remain untouched, like they were set in stone. If it were up to me, they would chisel at their own. And leave ours to be free, in a museum in the sky. That was always crystal blue, and angels didn't need to fly. To feel the admiration of the grounded, and our dreams were never considered foolish or unfounded. But little works of art, constructed in our heart. During a previous life, in which the future had taken part. But none of this matter to anyone but God. After all even His book is often met with disregard. So I shouldn't feel ashamed, or so quick to point the blame. At the ones who read, but can't pronounce my name.

Her Body's Speech

Fleeting thoughts, chasing a vapor's trace. The one he sought, left a paper in her place. The ink was smooth, but slow to dry. The words they soothe, but still they cry. In his mind so still, like echoed screams. in this room a chill, a slow-tempoed dream. The beats make colors, like impassioned red. Painted by the lovers, on a poorly fashioned bed. Pillowcases torn, below two curtains tattered. She feels reborn, whispered words leave her flattered. One breath dances, across the other's skin. Contemplating chances, of letting the other in. To the hearts we daily guard, from the swords and spears of wrong. To relax becomes this hard, only when your words and fears are strong. But these sheets of silk entomb, those in their closest reach. She embraced him in her womb, guiding him with her body's speech. But the talk is low, at a constant pace. There's so much to show, when looking at her face. Two bodies move as one, while the moon shines her approving light. For she isn't shy like the morning sun, she helps by removing all their fright. The sweat, it drips on the sheets, signs of effort in this dance. Still her body softly speaks, he listens close, leaves nothing to chance. With rapid thrusts and a gentle crash, their movements never seem to cease. She's nodding yes and in a flash, his love screams with a release. Emotions quickly pour inside, as she wraps her arms around. Softly weeping tears of pride, they both claim it's the rain that's coming down, outside.

CLYDE HURLSTON

The Artist's Touch

He slowly dipped the brush in paint, in the hopes of venting each complaint. So he splashed some shades of red, to mirror all the things that he once said. But his mood was a darkened blue, every time he thought of you. And your recycled compliments, aimed to inflate his confidence. Now his soul's in dire need, to watch these vibrant colors as they bleed. So the colors run like they had wept, his mind's as blank as the bed in which he slept. The pillows here are far from soft, oh his thoughts, he couldn't turn them off. As your face danced through his dreams, things are not as they would seem. For beauty hides the loss of decency, so in his mind you'll cease to be. Since now he knows what he must do, to finally drown these thoughts of you. And because he thinks of you too much, now you'll feel the artist's touch. And on the other side of a fateful coin, Is an unfolding tale that we will join. As a woman with a broken heart, watched as her world was torn apart. So she slowly dipped her pen in ink, to express the painful thoughts that she thinks. Then she scribbled words that he once used, as the ink and page became infused. And then her mood mirrored a phrase, that best described the wasted days. That she spent giving her love in vain, just to find the ending's still the same. For betrayal proves the loss of decency, so in her mind he'll cease to be. So now she knows what she must do, to finally drown these thoughts of you. And because she thinks of you too much, now you'll feel the artist's touch...

Two Birds On A Wire

As the room begins to spin, I feel the need for air. But I see your raise your hands, like you don't have a care. 'Cause you're just here to see, how far you can unwind. And you say I'm wound too tight, but you don't really mind. 'Cause there's something in your kiss, that I would die to feel. But since I've never felt like this, it's hard to tell what's real. So you can pinch my skin, and press your lips to mine. Then I will take my place, beside you on the vine. 'Cause we're just two birds on a wire, who will try their best. To try and take this higher, much higher than the rest. But girl I have to know, before the feeling's gone. Is the spark between us love, or is it what we're on. As the room begins to spin, I see you crack a smile. 'Cause the look upon my face, proves it's been awhile. Since I ever tried to fly, and get away from ground. While knowing if I fall, it may not make a sound. Like that tree inside the woods, when no one is around. But still I must relapse, to feel this love I've found. Is it coursing through the wire, or through your fingertips? 'Cause I feel a bit of fire, is held behind your lips. And girl, I'd gladly burn, like a suicidal moth. Since other girls and you, are made from different cloth. There's no other in this place, that I would rather have. And if you denied me this, I would go rather crazy, even mad. And choose that jacket white, then have them tie it tight. And try to give myself a hug, that felt like yours tonight. So you may make me beg, and you may make me plead. But I'll grovel for a chance, to taste that thing I need. So you can wave it in my face, or you can turn and wink.

But your love won't go to waste, so fuck what other people think. Leave rumors for the fools, and gossip for the old. 'Cause the things I'll do to you, are better left untold. There are some circuits made to trip, while others spark and fry. If they got the surge from you, that helped to get me high. Now I could light the whole damn town, without coming down. 'Cause there's lightning in my eyes, each time that you're around. So please remove conductors, and keep arms in the aisle. 'Cause if they want to bring us down, it just may take awhile....

Reach Skyward

Such power in my words. Like coals in a flaming heart. Granting my lease on a renewed lust for life. Acting as fuel in the veins of a rediscovered vigor. Using nothing but good intentions and a sharpened wit, I chip away at myself. Hoping to rid myself of the bitter disposition, that had cemented around me and become granite. But truth be told, I am not carved out of stone. Not in the way that society wishes me to be. And that is fine. Self-acceptance comes in time. The shame never takes root for long. It only passes through like a storm. See? You only master self-destruction with practice. Just as you only rebuild one stone at a time. For foundations never come in waves. No, they learn to reach skyward slowly.

A Royal Secret

It has taken time, to find comfort behind these eyes. And as I finally grasped this truth, I realized that there is a truly a king within my skin. And my throne? That lies deep within my bones. So after gazing deep into the abyss, the one buried deep inside the mind, it was then... that I swore eternal loyalty to my internal royalty and long will I reign.

The Quiet Lives Of Moths

What is it about forbidden things, that draws us like we're moths? Life could be a bed of roses, with satin sheets and still, we'd yearn for different cloths. Not content with happiness, we demand that danger be infused. While never knowing what we truly want, we even get mad when we're confused. But still, we continue searching letting our respective madness take the wheel. Technology has helped to make us numb, so is it wrong that we only wish to feel? For we could pinch ourselves until we're blue, and still not feel a thing. So we'll always curse the things that keep us safe, because it's only boredom that they bring.

Dreams Become Religion

As our day begin to die, our beds become the cross. On which our minds are sacrificed, and our temples turn and toss. But then we sink deeper into the black, and become so paralyzed; that the only things that seem to move, are our unsuspecting eyes. And then the sleep that scientists, have done their best to chart. Becomes the God within our lives, as all logic falls apart. And then emotions are oft revered, like the apostles they became. And memories are the gospel they recite, without a hint of shame. But this gospel is so very free, from the perception of those awake. That in this world the seas can wilt, and the skies can often break. And clouds rain down like shattered glass, while humans fly without their wings. As the shards of subconsciousness, pierce our skin until it stings. With the pain of disappointment, and the regrets we drown upon. But sometimes the sun comes shining through, and those emotions are finally gone. Leaving behind a welcomed trail, of the days so bittersweet. That our lives will often find a rug, Just to sweep the memories beneath. Because the world where our totems rule, will hate what we create. For they thrive on the selfishness, that our sedation will forsake. So as we resurrect each day, with the hopes of living out a dream. We see that people are more phony than, our projections would ever seem. So then we retreat to sleep each night, with the hopes of escaping just a bit. And it's on our precious little cross, that our bodies seem to fit. And friend I often wonder if the day, is the penance we have to pay. For being reborn each and every time, the sunlight fades away. So as the stars begin their turning out, I feel I must bid you all adieu. For there is a goddess I must dream about, and hope her arrival starts coming true...

CLYDE HURLSTON

A Writer Of A Different Sort

I was laying in my place, with a fiendish smile upon my face. And then a shining soul, who I'd helped to being whole. Looked down and said the things, that helped my pride to feel a sting. And thoughts began to race in head, as she smiled at me and said. "Can you tell I'm always watching? Can you tell that I observe? Your actions from a distance, in an effort to preserve. Myself inside an instance, because I see your way with words. They're so helpless to your pen, but I think it's what each one deserves. For their heads begin to spin, as you sway and move your pen. And they smile and let you in, and then they're never seen again. Gone missing in a world, still fueled by a boy who's meeting girl. And still they never realize, a true writer just won't compromise. So darling look within your chest, see the place your every breath will rest. And you'll see a heart that's draped in rust, thanks to it's disuse through your lust. 'Cause your wishing to finally prove, each time your pretty pen will move. That you can captivate a crowd, and all you have to do is whisper things aloud. And then their heads begin to spin, as you sway and move your pen. And they smile and let you in, and then they're never seen again. Gone missing in a world, still fueled by a boy who's meeting girl. And still they never realize, A true writer just won't compromise. You're not striking when you stand, with your feet on top of solid land. But put a pen inside your hand, and you become a different kind of man. Then you'll become a living dream, and you will write until I seem. Like a goddess on a throne, that you would die to make your own. And it's as your spilling ink, that I would then begin to think. That I've found my everything, and I'd hear angels start to sing. But now I see your halo's wrapped in thorns, to take attention off your horns. And though you're close to godly with a pen, there's a devil beneath your skin. So save your empty promises, for the crowd of fools and novices. They'll take everything you've got, but get thee from me, for love, I do know you not. And never again, will my head begin to spin, as you sway and move your pen. I won't smile or let you in, so I hope you're never seen again. And that you've gone missing in a world, still fueled by angry girls. Who woke up and realized, a true writer just won't compromise..."

CLYDE HURLSTON

The Writer's Block (1.0)

My inspiration's gone, the words won't hit the page. Like the lights were on, and the star won't hit the stage. But rationale it must coerce, each pretty line and darling verse. To finally leave their hiding place, 'cause we don't have the time to waste. As I lay beneath this writer's block, hearing sounds from quiet clocks. While the walls are closing in, and I can't reach my chosen pen. To bleed my tired soul of ink, despite the things that people think. And after all is said and dried, at least they can say I tried. Now imagination's running wild, and leaving us with strands. Like some hyperactive child, that nobody understands. Since focus makes the image blur, I can't find my way around. And as these little things occur, crumbled paper hits the ground. As I lay beneath this writer's block, hearing sounds from quiet clocks. While the walls are closing in, and I can't reach my chosen pen. To bleed my tired soul of ink, despite the things that people think. And after all is said and dried, at least they can say I tried. Now the public wants to read or hear, but I'm still paralyzed with fear. Because this page is bright and blank, and it's this block I have to thank. For choking thoughts before they come, leaving minds surprised and numb. But I can feel this block begin to lift, and fingertips have grazed my gift. As I lay beneath this writer's block, hearing sounds from quiet clocks. While the walls are closing in, and I can't reach my chosen pen. To bleed my tired soul of ink, despite the things that people think. And after all is said and dried, at least they can say I tried...

The Writer's Block (2.0)

How is it that ideas flow freely through my mind, like leaves atop a stream? And I can tell them to you vividly, as if I saw them in dream. But when it comes time to type them up, in the guise of a working script. Then my mind becomes as dry as a desert's sand, after the veil of mirage has slipped. I've read books that told me how, a writer should ply his trade. But tips and tricks are meaningless, when staring at the blankest page I've made. I'm fearing that I may go insane, if I journey further for a hint. For I've palmed my face so many times, I now fear that others may see its print. Frustration comes in many forms, but few as strong as this. So allow me to retreat to sleep, in my defeat, and in my forgotten dreams, may I find my bliss.

CLYDE HURLSTON

Flaws & Fractures

He who appears without flaw, is often a thrown stone away from fracture. But he who is intimate with his flaws, cannot ever be broken by them. And in turn, it is he who can endure and conquer, even the abyss within.

Symphonies

Can I be honest with you? I don't know how much I can take. The mystery is killing me. I need to know how you feel, darling. Daydreams wear off too quickly, and I need a prolonged high. I need you to see, that more than seas will rise, once this storm comes rolling in. I need to hear the symphonies, you hold within your breath. As the beast within me, pounds your shores like the tide. There will be no erosions here, baby. Just explosions. My fuse was lit the first time you looked at me. So what are you waiting for? And she said, "that'll do it."

CLYDE HURLSTON

Rapture

Oh, it's here I sit alone again, searching through a vacant mind. Watching clocks has gotten old, all it does is waste my time. But then I see the second hand, as it has to greet the first. And I swear it makes me think, that my outlook has gotten worse. I need to get from out this chair, step outside and grab some air. But every time I close my eyes, I see a flash of you and realize. That it seems I need a rapture, but not the kind from god. 'Cause I'm dying to escape, from a point of view that's flawed. And it seems I need a rapture, to finally save me from a mind. In which I have been captured, while waiting here for you to find. But here I sit alone again, lost in my thoughts of those. Who often failed to pass a glance, but that is the way it goes. And it's then I hear your voice, and I think, "my salvation's come". But it seems I can't rejoice, 'cause a mess is what I've become. Still, I need to get from out this chair, to step outside and grab some air. But every time I close my eyes, a part of me is compromised. 'Cause it seems I need a rapture, but not the kind from god. For I'm dying to escape, from a point of view that's flawed. And it seems I need a rapture, to finally save me from a mind. In which I have been captured, while waiting here for you to find. But here I am alone again, with my hands entrenched in hair. I've stared into the abyss so long, I've discovered all the wonders there. But all that's good does not compare, to the thought of seeing you. And if you said you'd save me now, I'd try my hand at believing you. Would find a way around my name, and clean the mess that I became. Waiting here's become the norm, and I'm far too calm inside the storm. But with no one here to pull me out, and so I've gotten intimate with doubt. But all she does is put me down, while pointing out you're not around.

And I think the saddest part, is that I know she's right. But then she starts to look like me, when held up to the candlelight. But as that flame tries reaching high, and the wick begins to die. I wonder if you wonder why, I long to feel your temple try. To hide each quake that it might make, after bending 'til it's close to break. Your valleys I will not forsake, for I long to be your sweet mistake. Still, I need to get from out this chair, to step outside and grab some air. But every time I close my eyes, I fear you won't become my prize. 'Cause it seems I need a rapture, but not the kind from god. For I'm dying to escape, from a point of view that's flawed. And it seems I need a rapture, to save me from a mind. In which I have been captured, while waiting here for you to find. That a glance at you, my precious gift, is sure to help these spirits lift. And I try not to stare, but can't resist, though you're unaware, that I even do exist. And darling, that's no fault of yours, but I can't walk through unopened doors. So please light the way, into your heart, and I'll slide right in, then play my part. But there have been far too many roosters, In the fabled, house of hens. And far too many demons, hiding in the guise of friends. Dear, I understand, this dilemma true, these foolish boys, have done no good for you. But I'm still overlooked, and in your view. with no one to love, and nothing to do. But to get from out this chair, to step outside and grab some air. But every time I close my eyes, I hope you will finally realize. That it seems I need a rapture, but not the kind from god. For I'm dying to escape, from a point of view that's flawed. And it seems I need a rapture, to finally save me from a mind. In which I have been captured, while waiting here for you to find. Just how much I need you...

A Writer's Dream

I have dreamed a writer's dream, but not of the sleeping kind. Buried deep within the soul, where the weeping often find. Apart of themselves they've lost, under ashes of their guilt. An effigy of sorts, in remembrance of what love had built. Gazing at the stars, that tonight are not in sight. The clouds have become obese, and they're eating up the light. It is in this dream I stand, alone in a baron field. With the grass dancing in the wind, and the breeze I've longed to feel. The thunder mirrors applause, from a filled up concert hall. As the sure-handed drops of rain, finally lose their grip and fall. As they plummet towards the Earth, they gently kiss my face. And for once I feel alive, in this most God-forsaken place. In the distance there's a figure, moving slowly in the dark. I cannot see their steps, but I can hear the beating of their heart. Much like a whispering drum, the volume is dying to increase. Their cloak is blowing in the wind, because the breeze has yet to cease. Toward me the figure slowly moves, and they're raising up their arm. And I can't seem to figure out, if they intend to do me harm. I touch the figure's extended hand, to feel their gentle skin. It's as soft as an angel's wings, and the color of porcelain. The stranger removes their hood, to reveal their identity. A goddess in her human form, is what the Lord has sent to me. Softly, I caress her face, her eyes are glowing like the moon. She said, "Beloved, I will end your despair, and I will end it soon." She removed her darkly-colored cloak, that she had chose to wear. And then she slowly revealed to me, that nothing was under there. Her body was soft and firm, like beauty in the purest form. And then she gave herself to me, beneath this violent storm. As I lay down in the friendly dirt, she straddled my exhausted legs. To release in her all my hurt, is for what she softly begs. As she's rocking back and forth, I begin to feel reborn. I can feel her slowly mend, a soul that was long since torn. Her movements often changed in speed, as I struggled to adjust. It's been years since I felt this way, can you tell me if it's love or lust. For how can you love someone, who was previously unknown? Was she truly sent to me, so that I may call her my own? Her movements finally reached a peak, followed by a gentle crash. Neither one of us could speak, and it was over in a flash. She softly kissed my lips, and said your pain is inside of me. As I felt her fingertips, I felt my mind divide in three. Part of it couldn't accept the fact, that my pain was finally gone. The middle part did rejoice, and said it's been too long. The third part finally woke me up, from sleeping soundly in my bed. And if that was just a dream, why do I hear her voice echo in my head? Then I felt the slightest touch, brush against my feet. I looked at the covers I was in, to see someone underneath. I pulled those covers back, to see my dream had come to life. She said, "if you don't stop waking me, I'll never be your wife." And it was then we shared a laugh, but she was blind to my delight. To see that dreams really do come true, and mine finally did that night. But if this encounter was another dream, then I beg you leave me be. Because I would gladly stay asleep, if she is sleeping next to me. And as she slept deeply beneath my arm, I thought to reveal her name. But instead, I'll keep that to myself, and just tell you that God is in the rain...

Is Unrequited A Requisite?

Another year is drawing to a close. The hourglass is striking, the all too familiar pose. Draining down, running out. Showing me that time, is just another thing. I am forced to do without. But that is fine, all is well. The year has left the same old tale to tell. Living should feel like Heaven, and not like I'm penetrating hell. The sweat upon my brow, is showing here and now, that the burdens on my back. Allow me to mirror Atlas, but I fear I'm going to crack. But that is fine, all is well. But as I sit upon a lonely throne, I wish to wear the crown of thorns I own. Hoping that the blood it drew to pour, would hide my tears, along with everything and more. And yet I don't. The crown is on the ground. The dirty place, where my scepter could be found. For my iron fist has wilted, and left the open hand that's bound. To hold my face, as if, it is the only place, where it could come to rest, without shame. Without the shame of being seen, the shame of being so very far from clean. And the bitterness of being miles and miles away, from the center of your every dream. The world will turn. But I will only sit. And yearn. And I know you will wear a puzzled look, wondering just what on Earth I mean. But if you will sit and rest awhile, I will use words instead of ink, to calmly paint the scene. Did you know there was once a laundry list of things, that I would die to do to you. And I would execute the acts, one by one, until that fabled list was through. And I would've described your sweetest taste, to any soul with ears. And if you cried to me, in sweet delight, I would slowly drink your tears. But only if you liked that sort of thing. And not preferred them wiped instead. I swear you will never know the depths or heights, you have reached inside my head. No, you'll continue drifting through the days, counting hours 'til you see. Someone who is at the very least, a lesser shade of me. And though their exterior may draw your eyes, the interior hides the truth. But sadly still, you'll never learn, we'll just hear you chalk it up to youth. But please believe what I observe, contains no judgment in the least. Dear, I just tire of your worshiping, those who should follow behind your leash. But amongst the cavalcade of thoughts, running quickly through my brain. Lies a central, God forsaken theme, that often causes me to then complain. The words, "is unrequited a requisite?", have become my clarion call. Wondering if my feelings are not returned, just so I can feel anything at all. Whether it must be disappointment, or a tinge of bitter rage. My heart has been a dormant corpse, lying at the bottom of its' cage. Oh, merciful Creator, are my Expectations Great? Must I be like fabled Pip, tell me, must we share a fate? Or am I like the foolish brute, who rang the bells of Notre Dame? Thinking if Esmeralda spoke of love, she would surely say my name. Or maybe I'm like Orsino and, I must wait to count the nights. Until the number gets to twelve, and Olivia's square within my sights. Or maybe I should be thankful, I've never loved Charlotte 'til she wed. 'Cause I'd've ended up like poor Werther, with an ending better left unread. And surely poor Cyrano knows, the taste of longing for Roxane. When he let bumbling Christian use his words, 'til he was proved a mortal man. But dear, do you see my point in this? Or should the poet wax until you're sure? That he's not asking you to share in wedded bliss, but to merely look this way some more. And I will never ask you to do a thing, that I would not do for you. But I think Cupid's either drunk or blind, for his arrow's not piercing through. The walls you've chosen to erect, to keep out the souls who look like me. And I could use my hands to tear them down, but that ending's unlikely. So maybe I'll have to speak until my voice, becomes a whisper not a roar. Maybe then I can rejoice, for being near the one I do adore. But I feel that endings such as this, are better left in stories still unread. Because men like me do die alone, so I fear these words were better left unsaid. But maybe fate will prove me wrong, though it's more than that I doubt. Now, I'll beg you to leave me to my lonesome love, and please remember as you leave, to blow the lonely candle out...

CLYDE HURLSTON

Hypergraphia

Strength is just the touted twin, of the weakness that I feel within. That's displayed upon a stage so grim, my thoughts will give way to whims. So as I'm reaching for a virgin page, the beast's about to leave its' cage. Brimming to it's eyes with rage, and the disposition of a lonely sage. With an overwhelming urge to write, about the ways I thought were right. But when I look inside your eyes tonight, I've come to find I've lost my light. Forgive me... For the darkness ever filling me, I get off on times you're feeling weak. And as I watch you fight to speak, the well within your eyes begins to leak. But that doesn't make me feel a thing, I've no sympathy left to bring. So even if you're inclined to sing, just know that I'm ignoring everything. 'Cause I have an overwhelming urge to write, about the ways I thought were right. But when I look inside your eyes tonight, I've come to find I've lost my light. Forgive me... For never thinking that you'd choose, to give up life as my sacred muse. 'Cause if I knew I lit your fuse, I would've used much lighter hues. And turned that sky back to blue, so you'd know every word was true. But now it seems our art is through, since someone sunk their claws into you. So now I have an overwhelming urge to write, about the ways I thought were right. But when I look inside your eyes tonight, I've come to find I've lost my light. Forgive me... For not being more vocal dear, and saying the words you want to hear. But even great minds are choked with fear, and feel the burdens of each yesteryear. When our gifts were often met, by reactions we'd as soon forget. And as we siphon fuel from regret, we haven't seen his grace or kingdom yet. But we have an overwhelming urge to write, about the ways we thought were right. But when I look inside your eyes tonight, I've come to find I've lost my light. And maybe someday... I'll forgive me...

Deny Your Father

It's been said by those around, you've been forced to live this way. But dear I don't believe, that this is how it has to stay. For each day we see, is a concealed opportunity. To improve and build upon, what we have before all is said and gone. You're too afraid that you'll falter, so you won't step down from the altar. Oh, dear it's easy to see, there's more you could be. But you're content with this life, so I doubt that you'll bother. To start denying your name, or even denying your father. It's been said by those around, that you have a certain way. With those who've come to see, your temple on this day. For each night we see, is a concealed opportunity. To tear down and then remove, our guards like we have something left to prove. You're too afraid that you'll falter, so you won't step down from the altar. Oh, dear it's easy to see, there's more that you could be. But you're content with this life, so I doubt that you'll bother. To start denying your name, or even denying your father. So it's best to start pressing the issue, since no one will miss you. When there'll be some other face, to fill your vacant place. For each day we see, is a true gift my dear. But the things that you need, will never be found here. Especially if you're too afraid that you'll falter, and you won't step down from the altar. Oh, dear it's easy to see, this is all you will be. 'Cause you're content with this life, so I doubt that you'll bother. And you won't deny your name, much less deny your father!

The Ecstasy Of Self

Now when I look so deep inside, my inner Hyde no longer hides. And it's then I often see, the things I've been denied. For suppression made me weak, and too afraid to speak. But now I'll soon enjoy, all this havoc I will wreak. 'Cause I use to think so much of life, that I've forgotten how to live. And now my inner bitterness, is the only gift I have to give. But darling, that will change today, as I improve my health. By my finally going through, this ecstasy of self. Now I've seen the anima within, and I've shown persona out. Oh, shadow come and show me things, that I've long forgot about. And then I will beg the id, to fully manifest in me. And make me the kind of man, I've always wished to be. 'Cause I use to think so much of life, that I've forgotten how to live. And now my inner bitterness, is the only gift I have to give. But darling, that will change today, as I improve my health. By my finally going through, this ecstasy of self. And for such a lack of subtlety, persona will have to suffer me. As I pierce the flesh of yesterday, teaching no to say yes today. For now I'll never be denied, things to inflate my wretched pride. As I see yet another femme fatale, that I would die just to be inside. 'Cause my persona was so very flawed, that I'd have to hide my wants. But in my shadow I'm a demi-god, that Satan never tempts or taunts. Because He's come to recognize, that my veil has slipped away. So it's here before our very eyes, that I will transcend the older way. 'Cause I use to think so much of life, that I've forgotten how to live. And now my inner bitterness, is the only gift I have to give. But darling, that will change today, as I improve my health. By my finally going through, this ecstasy of self. And now this pleasure principle, is a dogma in my eyes. That I will follow blindly 'til, I lay hands upon my prize. And I will never second guess, the things I wish to do. Until I'm labeled as the best, that's ever been inside of you. So girl, consult your animus, and you'll find that I'm for real. Unless the misery life is handing us, is all you wish to feel. 'Cause I've felt it everyday, until I chose to quit. And now my shadow is a flame, that's forever remaining lit.

The Fool Who Waits

Beyond these tempting gates, lies the paradise of lore. But it's said the fool who waits, shall never past the door. So I'm staring at your garden, love. With trees not bearing fruit. While vibrant leaves just hang above, that tree mirrors my pursuit. Like that time I took the wheel, on a search for something real. But all I ever found, was cold and unforgiving ground. Yet still I drive today, to try and find a way. To get beyond those gates, because I'm that fool who waits. And I thought I held the key, within all I had to give. But thanks to intangibles, outside's where I had to live. And this downward slide, that friendship's forced to take. Just won't slow down, or even try to brake. Like that time I took the wheel, on a search for something real. But all I ever found, was cold and unforgiving ground. Yet still I drive today, to try and find a way. To get beyond those gates, because I'm that fool who waits. And as I head downhill, I take a little glance. My eyes begin to fill, in hopes there is a chance. That I'll survive the plunge, though a part of me will not. So I hold on tight, and give it everything I've got. Like that time I took the wheel, on a search for something real. But all I ever found, was cold and unforgiving ground. Yet still I drive today, to try and find a way. To get beyond those gates, because I'm that fool who waits. Now it seems another has the key, to the paradise of lore. But that fool moves with haste, and gets far beyond the door. And it seems the rib I sacrificed, was used to pick the lock. And the blank look upon my face, mirrors the expression on the clock. So as the sands slip through, the center of the glass. I take my solace in the fact, that paradise will never last. But deep inside I think, that it'd be nice to feel. The warm embrace of grace, and the salvation it conceals. But now it's time I took the wheel, and search for something real. Even though all I've ever found, was cold and unforgiving ground. Yet still I drive today, to try and find a way. To get beyond those gates, 'cause for far too long, I've been that fool who waits....

A DEBT PAID IN INK

The Bitter Loss Of Eden

It seems a slice of heaven, is all that I'm allowed. So why do I voice displeasure, each time I speak aloud? It was then my blossomed, living rib, slowly turned to me and said. "Adam, you are not alone, for these thoughts are in my head." Then we were greeted by a serpent, who seemed to share a point of view. And stoked our burning temperaments, by revealing what we had to do. So now we're reaching for an apple, on this once forbidden tree. For it's often in our plainest sight, where things are hidden constantly. So we shared the smallest, little bite, thinking all was right and fine. But we were sure about to see, how wrong we were in time. 'Cause the skies began to darken, and a booming voice was heard. As we began to tremble, for having disobeyed His word. Then I glanced behind our bodies, hoping the snake would clear our name. But the silver tongue had disappeared, leaving faster than he came. So then expulsion was the penance, as we began to fall from grace. Some wonder was it worth it, losing heaven for a taste. But it seems we're only human, so mistakes will bring us shame. But if He made us in His image, should we be the ones to blame? Since we are living out the plans, He has laid out for our life. But since I bit this stupid apple, I introduced this world to strife. And now most are blaming Eve, though the biggest bite was mine. And while these leaves are used for cover, I still feel naked in my mind. For this mistake that we have made, will echo throughout eternity. And we'll be painted as the villains, or at least fools most certainly. And this impending infamy, does possess a bitter sting. But it can't compare to losing Eden, for that place meant everything...

CLYDE HURLSTON

Skill At Sin

Place your pen upon my cheek, and write the words you've often read. Because you seem to know the things, that I haven't even said. But I'll place my lips upon your cheek, to taste the tears you've often cried. 'Cause it will cause your face to shine, after the pain has gone and dried. And where we go from here, only the hands of fate will know. But knowing you'll be there, is as far as my faith will go. And no, I haven't learned to pray, for things to go my way. 'Cause every time I hit my knees, my skill at sin is on display. And now my tongue will write the words, that'll make you fall in love. And I'll never have to promise that, I won't place a soul above. The pedestal you rest upon, for all the world to see. Since you're just a soul to them, and only mean the world to me. And where we go from here, only the hands of fate will know. But knowing you'll be there, is as far as my faith will go. And no, I haven't learned to pray, for things to go my way. 'Cause every time I hit my knees, my skill at sin is on display. So open your sweet world, show me the path to travel. Place your hands in my hair dear, let your worries unravel. Inhibitions are killed slow, when the sacrifice is willing. And your love is a sweet well, that time has been filling. So baby don't think, just close your eyes and let me drink. I'll take you to the brink, show you Heaven between each blink. No, baby don't think, just close your eyes and let me drink. I'll take you to the brink, show you Heaven between each blink. And where we go from here, only the hands of fate will know. But knowing you'll be there, is as far as my faith will go. And no, I haven't learned to pray, for things to go my way. 'Cause every time I hit my knees, my skill at sin is on display. Girl, these words I fought to say, should prove I'm made for you. And these skills that I display, were given to me, to take your every pain away...

CLYDE HURLSTON
The Heaviest Of Heads

If my written words were waves, in an ocean of intent. Then it's no surprise your shore, is where they often went. For I've always longed to be, the place on which you chose to rest. After you dropped the heavy anchor, that resides within your chest. But they say the heaviest of heads, always sits beneath the crown. But after everything is said, it's your heart that weighs you down. 'Cause it truly is your compass, and helps you find your way. But you can lay it down for once, and not save this world today. Darling, there will be a time, when they have to save themselves. Because apathy's the reason, they dug the grave themselves. But I will never try to stop you, from caring in the least. When it's your suffering for them, that I truly aim to cease. 'Cause the day you fail to help them, is when the blame will lay. Squarely at the doorstep, from which they were never turned away. And they you'll be a martyr, for the most beautiful of sins. Like trying to make your means, finally justify their ends. And they say the heaviest of heads, always sits beneath the crown. But after everything is said, it's your heart that weighs you down. 'Cause it truly is your compass, and helps you find your way. But you can lay it down for once, and not save this world today. But I won't discourage your courage, nor will I ever seek to impede. This righteous sort of life, you've made the choice to lead. But it's okay to take a day, to devote just to you. After you feel that your mission, has been seen until it's through. And I'll still praise your resolve, 'cause your actions have always shown. The price for sacrifice, and the strength of flesh and bone.

And if there truly is a God, He can look down from His cloud. 'Cause I'll still look to you, and say these words aloud. They say the heaviest of heads, always sits beneath the crown. But after everything is said, it's your heart that weighs you down. 'Cause it truly is your compass, and helps you find your way. But you can lay it down for once, and not save this world today.

CLYDE HURLSTON

The Things That Make You

In life there is a place, that most don't wish to see. But friend it's what I have to face, and where I'll always be. So you can fight your craving, it's a spot I deserve. So quell your thoughts of saving, you'd do better to preserve. The things that make you, mean so much to me. These things should take you, to where you need to be. 'Cause you've held me up here, for too long in my view. And these are the things, that make you too good to be true. In life there is a place, where I spend most of my days. But there's still a pretty face, that earns all of my praise. So you can hide your envy, but still I'll make her mine. 'Cause she'll lovingly defend me, from things inside my mind. Oh girl, these are the things that make you, mean so much to me. These things should take you, to where you need to be. 'Cause you've held me up here, for too long in my view. And these are the things, that make you too good to be true. Being difficult, comes so easily. But it's your touch, that brings an ease to me. So you can tell your friends, and you can say it loud. I'm a fool for you, and that was stated proud. In life there is a place, where I'd die to be. And it's made a sacred space, by you laying next to me. So you can rest your head, and you can close your eyes. I'll move my tongue instead, and help you kiss the skies. Oh girl, these are the things that make you, mean so much to me. And these are the things that should take you, to where you need to be. 'Cause you've held me up here, for too long in my view. And these are the things, that make you too good to be true. Oh girl, these are the things that make you, taste divine to me. Oh, these hands would break through, concrete just to see. If you loved the things, that this man could do. 'Cause baby those are the things, that make you too good to be true.

CLYDE HURLSTON

Try Your Hand At Sin

The crowd of sheep are roaming, with their shepherd square in view. But that smile of yours is showing, like it always seems to do. And so you go about your day, to find comfort in routine. But with eyes as trained as mine, the truth can rarely go unseen. Darling, pretend these words of mine, are apples on a tree. Dangling here before your eyes, for all the world to see. And before you take a bite of them, know you don't have to share. And if you need an ear to bend, know that mine are always there. But I know it's in your nature, to show the world your best. And ignore the growing pain, pounding hard within
your chest. And as fear gives way to rage, you debate on acting out. 'Cause your co-star back at home, is now severely lacking clout. And dear I hope you won't regret, what you were made to do. 'Cause you'll see how good it feels, when you aren't afraid of you. And when right starts feeling wrong, and your wits are at their end. It's then I'll encourage you, to try your hand at sin. 'Cause all you wanted was the love, you were promised from the start. But now a player on the stage, won't play his fabled part. And so you start to wonder, if they should be recast. 'Cause a rave-reviewed performance, just won't seem to last. And with auditions drawing near, I hope you'll call my name. 'Cause I'd keep on standing by, without a hint of shame. And if you could walk inside my mind, would it delight you much to know. That I've thought of bending you, if every position you could go. And my thoughts are often dark, with things better done at night. But my dear I do believe, that you'd taste better in the light. Of the proudest set of candles,

that would ever hold a flame. As if bestowed to us in kind, and Prometheus were to blame. Oh darling, would it make you blush. To know of all the times, that I've often got a rush. As I viewed you from behind, wishing I could place you on a desk, and introduce my tongue to you. As you'd recite your breathless prayers, 'til the moment I was through. With your fingers in my hair, acting like waves inside my locks. I'd rarely come up for air, as you forgot the ticking of the clocks. But these are merely thoughts, that I've often held at bay. Because there's a ring upon your hand, and you barely look my way. And you bare no fault in this, for I'm a sight that's better left. To eyes that are truly sore, or to those that hold their breath. Oh, there I go again, rambling at the mind. Hoping to circle back in thought, until the point of view I find. Will often rhyme enough, for you to place value on the words. That I'd probably never speak, but that your set of ears deserve. 'Cause I'd bet dollars to the dimes, that you don't hear those words at home. So you wander lost through crowds, wondering how you can feel alone. As you journey to the closest fence, looking for a brighter shade of green. When it's compared to the dying grass, that you have often seen. And it's a shame to me, that an angel with your wings. Still longs to receive the light, that she often brings. To those closest to her heart, or merely in her radius. And while some may give you love, girl, I only wish to activate your lust. But if thrusts gave way to hugs, and our positions weren't for sport. I'd gladly make a queen of you, to help me rule the court. That's truly filled with jesters, playing games throughout the day. When the saddest part of all, the biggest clown is in your bed today. But that's no fault of mine, and truly none of yours. You only wished to live the dream, every little girl adores. But now you've grown into a sight, I'd describe as goddess to a tee. And if you ever feel the need to cheat, don't be afraid to call on me. Because I'll truly never mind, if your relationship is flawed. Because I only want to make you smile, before I make you scream for God. And I hope you won't regret, what you were made to do. 'Cause you'll see how good it feels, when you aren't afraid of you. And when right starts feeling wrong, and your wits are at their end. It's then I'll encourage you, to try your hand at sin...

A DEBT PAID IN INK

Ceiling Height

A gentle rose in screaming sun, leaning in to kiss the light. But the modern clock's a clever one, leaving day without time to fight. But as darkness came she proudly stood, beautiful and motionless. For it's said still waters often run, deeper than the ocean is. But then she turned to me and said... You're so wrong for being right, but my state of mind is ceiling height. And I won't come down until I feel, your razor tongue will let me heal. And you're so wrong for bleeding me, when other souls are needing me. Now my wound's beyond repair, and you seem beyond a care. So there I stood with open mouth, as she looked down her nose at me. From a point of view I never had, you know how the ground can be. But I reached up to grab her feet, then she kicked my hand away. Because she saw I'd never change, and thought it best to fly not stay. So she opened up the window, and I thought I heard her say... You're so wrong for being right, but my state of mind is ceiling height. And I won't come down until I feel, your razor tongue will let me heal. And you're so wrong for bleeding me, when other souls are needing me. Now my wound's beyond repair, and you seem beyond a care. And as a bridge began to burn, the ashes swirled and filled the air. It seems like she had finally learned, to release her thoughts of pure despair. Because biting on your bottom lip, will only keep the words at bay. When darling what you have to do, is just say whatever you will say. And I will have no other choice, but to learn I had to let you go. Because there was a better side of me, that I never had the heart to show. So I'll bury it along with pain, and pretend like I don't care at all.

But I'll choose to sit by the phone, hoping that she'll choose to call. 'Cause there's an open hole inside my life, that I will never truly fill. But her last words echoed in my ears, through a window open still. Like when she turned to me and said... You're so wrong for being right, but my state of mind is ceiling height. And I won't come down until I feel, your razor tongue will let me heal. And you're so wrong for bleeding me, when other souls are needing me. Now my wound's beyond repair, and you seem beyond a care. So now I hit my knees in shame, like one seeking penance does. And I think, Lord if she only knew, just how wrong she was...

A DEBT PAID IN INK

Passion. Restrained.

In these wayward centuries, my love is like the tide. And I've built myself a dam, to help keep this force inside. For I wish to keep it in, so it doesn't greet your eyes. Or escape these bitter walls, to leave its' mark upon your lives. But it's said that there are those, who wish to brave the climb. And will scale the face of my defense, just to see what they will find. So I guess it's best for me, to sit bound and wish them well. But if I was asked for inner truth, it'd be a different tale I'd tell. Because I don't want the outer world, to see inside of me. And get a glimpse of inner gifts, their God's provided me. But I'd be remiss if I don't admit, there's one who will succeed. And she'll destroy what I enjoyed, then give me what I need. And that's the dismantling, of this wall I've come to love. And stone by stone will kiss the ground, while more are diving from above. Then I watch her stand triumphantly, while smiling just a bit. And I realize the things she wants, are the things she'll often get. So if she wants the better parts, still hidden behind this wall. She better brace, prepare to face, the raging wave that's sure to fall. Through the cracks and gaping holes, she has made with loving hands. And while she tries to hold her own, I think she finally understands. That it's best for her to wish with care, because one day she may receive. And there is a certain phrase I'll say, when I'm sure she will believe. Because my love was once a river, now an ocean since it's bloomed. And my doubts are like the darkened clouds, that tell the day it's doomed. But this girl is like the morning sun, that shines through clouds of mine. And I asked for reasons why, which she revealed in time. And she said that it's because, I was the man inside her dreams. And she believed my uttered phrase, and comprehended what it means. But I made her jump through flaming hoops, and she never once complained. For she thinks my love is better felt, after my passion's been restrained. But now my love is flowing free, and it's hers and hers alone. For she proved the better path, is best taken when it's shown. And I am forever grateful. For her...

A DEBT PAID IN INK

What Once They Called

At the mercy of the winter winds, there seems to be a sacred fight. Mother Nature's raised her ire, against the butterfly in flight. Flapping both her tired wings, she sighs as if to save the rest. Of the breath she'll surely need, to ease the pain inside her chest. And what once they called a butterfly, is just another moth to die. Deep inside a darling flame, beneath a God you'd hardly blame. For her hurting heart that slowly beat, to the rhythm of a bitter name. 'Cause in these cold and lonely times, solace is what the word became. But if you ask she'll tell you no, yet the lashes of her eyes say yes. For they're the ones who caught the tears, that almost fell and died upon her breast. Since what once they called a butterfly, is just another moth to die. Deep inside a darling flame, beneath a God you'd hardly blame. For the fact her latest love affair, has left her with another scar. That she'll have to hide from view, it's how she made it through this far. But darling's pushing further still, like she'll defy the very gods. Who placed these things inside her path, to further complicate her odds. And what once they called a butterfly, is just another moth to die. Deep inside a darling flame, beneath a God you'd hardly blame. For the fact that she has never found, more than a fleeting glimpse of love. And her concerns are weighted things, that she can't seem to rise above. But if she were somehow to shake, free of the things that keep her here. Then the clouds should part to give her space, where she could fly so free and clear. But what once they called a butterfly, is just another moth to die. Deep inside a darling flame, beneath a God you'd hardly blame.

For the fact that they call this butterfly, only when it suits them best. So she'll fly high above me now, since she thinks that I'm just like the rest...

A DEBT PAID IN INK

Confessions Trapped In Breath

Today is just another day, that I've been blessed to see. But it's living out each one, that's made this mess of me. But since I'm awake again, beneath an avalanche of stress. I feel there are so many things, that I should confess. Like how there is a tidal wave, of tears behind my eyes. And if I said the reason why, I'd be adding to my lies. Because the reason that I'd reveal, has escaped my reach again. So fallacies are all I can muster up, when digging deep within. And this skin I'm sitting in, is withering and cold. But it would bloom again someday, is what I'm often told. They say the only thing it needs, is tender, loving care. But after searching under lonely rocks, what I seek is never there. And to say that I'm surprised, is far from accurate. 'Cause when you look the way I do, it's the best you'll ever get. But at least the blessed day will come, when I will find some peace. Maybe then the waves that we've discussed, will finally start to cease. But I confess that I daily feel, the waves behind my eyes. And if I said the reason why, I'd be adding to my lies. Because the reason that I'd reveal, has escaped my reach again. So fallacies are all I can muster up, when digging deep within. For fallacies digest the best, when they're offered to the world. And they'll then become the truth, when their feathered wings unfurl. And they are carried by the wind, like confessions trapped in breath. Until the breeze feels its' interest wane, and the lies plummet to their death. Because my confessions are best unheard, for they depress the ones who hear. That this world is just turning cell, with unseen bars that keep us here. In the fettered states we lie, or at least that's the way it's seen. When looking through these eyes of mine, that this life was just a dream. But it's more like a nightmare friend, that has been left upon repeat. And has morphed into some created beast, that I must rise up to defeat. But alas this confession's spun, far beyond my mere control. So until my eternal sleep has begun, I think it best to try and save my soul. So I will leave these confessions, as the muted burdens I will keep. While I wish what's best for you, and try to find some solace as I sleep...

A DEBT PAID IN INK

CLYDE HURLSTON

The Joys Of Martyrdom

Deep inside a sea of sheets, a quiet sermon's what she speaks. Hymns are sung by two heartbeats, as passing seconds feel like weeks. His arms outstretched in sweet delight, wrapped in the legs of his savior. He felt two souls became one tonight, as he slowly gave himself to her. And she said... "I'm so glad that you could come, and feel the joys of martyrdom. Tonight you will be born again, as the nails impale your skin." Deep inside a darkened room, his fears were introduced to death. Desires will explode and bloom, causing gasps and shortened breath. His raging lust then turns to greed, as blood poured out the sacrifice. And as his want became a need, he was the lamb that paid the price. As she said... "I'm so glad that you could come, and feel the joys of martyrdom. Tonight you will be born again, as the nails impale your skin. Yes, I'm so glad that you could come, and feel the joys of martyrdom. Now the world will sing your praise, and worship all your godly ways." And he was quick to look down and reply, "Will you justify the pain I feel? And prove to me that God is real? Or will you say that I denied you? And poured my hate so deep inside you..." There was a man without a cross, who finally gained from what he lost. Inside a fog of welcomed sins, her nails pierced his weakest skin. Blood slowly poured from all his wounds, her eyes lit up like the stars and moons. So now he'll feel this sweet rebirth, thanks to a girl that knew his worth. Who lovingly smiled before she said... "I'm so glad that you could come, and feel the joys of martyrdom. Tonight you will be born again, as the nails impale your skin. Love, I'm so glad that you could come, and feel the joys of martyrdom. Now the world will sing your praise, And worship all your godly ways..." And he replied, "You justified the pain I feel, and proved to me that God is real. So please don't say that I denied you, as I pour my love so deep inside you..."

CLYDE HURLSTON

A Fashion That's Precise

The thought of you alone, is so pleasing to the mind. Like a sight is to the eyes, or ears finding sound sublime. But the question then becomes, what can be taken from their sum? Is there a part of you in me, that I simply can't outrun? Must I submit? Must I kneel? Even bow before your grace? As my inner thoughts combine, to make a mosaic of your face. As your name drapes the walls, like the finest form of art. That was framed, then became, picture perfect in my heart. Darling girl, I won't lie, I thought alone is how I'd die. 'Til you came in, to begin, to just inspire me to try. So breathe your life, or be my wife. Do anything you wish. And give me time, I'll tell you why, my fabled wish is this. Girl, tell me anything, make any word suffice. Rub my name across your tongue, in a fashion that's precise. Say it with a dash of pride, as if the owner is your own. And I will take you in my arms, and place you on the throne. 'Cause if you think it through, you'd know I think of you. Whether my eyes are open wide, or there's darkness in my view. I think of you, I think of you. I think of only you. I think of you, I think of you. What else am I to do? But humbly drift beneath your waist, to grant myself a taste. For you possess the holy grail, and I shall worship it with haste. But please believe, I won't deceive, I'd rather prove my worth. My first is now in last, you're the only woman on this Earth. If you look, inside my book, and read upon the page. My heart and soul, lacked control, for they were shackled in a cage. That could not been seen, or even felt, but it was so very hard to move. Until you came through, well to do, with a word and touch to soothe.

A DEBT PAID IN INK

The inner storm, that was the norm, and grown to be the sight. That I despised, before my eyes, got to close and end the night. So baby girl, please rejoice, you were my favorite choice. And you won't doubt sincerity, if you listen to my voice, when I say... Girl, tell me anything, make any word suffice. Rub my name across your tongue, in a fashion that's precise. Say it with a dash of pride, as if the owner is your own. And I will take you in my arms, and place you on the throne. 'Cause if you think it through, you'd know I think of you. Whether my eyes are open wide, or there's darkness in my view. I think of you, I think of you. I think of only you. I think of you, I think of you. What else am I to do? But thank you for the things, you never noticed that you did. And the happiness it brings, I only felt it as a kid. So now I display it with a pride, that I really feel inside. For you embody all things, a man should never be denied. Girl, your walk, oh girl, your talk, brings such life inside a room. That fate would probably like to cast, its' newest bride and groom. But before we get that far, I have to thank you here and now. Because you organized my pain, then somehow cleared it out. Now I can tell you anything, and make any word suffice. For you filled my inner void, in a fashion that's precise. And it's with a dash of pride, that I say the owner is your own. So I will take you in my arms, and I will place you on the throne. 'Cause if you think it through, you'd know I think of you. Whether my eyes are open wide, or there's darkness in my view. I think of you, I think of you. Girl, I think of only you. I think of you, I think of you. What else am I to do? But thank you...

CLYDE HURLSTON
The Penrose Stairs

Darling, won't you spin your top, and tell the world if I'm awake. For I wish to lie beside you ever still, and applaud each breath you take. But your beauty's being held within, a metaphoric maze beneath your breast. That any man will have to brave, to find where the heart is said to rest. But as I dip below the tangible, I see no keeper creature of the lore. For I'm not sure that I'd survive, an encounter with the minotaur. But now that I'm within your world, I must fight to find my ground. Because it seems your lovers past, have left this place so turned around. So I'm walking on your ceilings dear, while I long to touch your floors. Walking through the windows as, I stare intently through your doors. For I investigate this blooming world, filled with vines to guide my way. As I hear you sing in Shepard tones, the sweetest things you have to say. And while your siren's song may well entice, my reasons have wavered not. For I can find delight in failure's grasp, if I know I gave it all I've got. And that is what I wish to give, to you and you alone. As I climb the penrose stairs, that you've built here on your own. To protect your precious parts, from the unfaithful hands of those. Who don't appreciate the petal's touch, so they meet the thorns and curse the rose. But I am not like those gardeners, no matter how much you may believe. That I would plant my seed in fertile ground, just to take a bow and leave. So you can put down your weary shield, and sheathe your sharpened sword. For there's just a heart upon this sleeve, where the others' tricks were stored. And though I'm not without my wiles, it's at your mercy I remain. And I've spent this time below your heel, without an ounce of shame. But to say that I won't move, would be a spoken lie. For I wish to be the sun that shines, through your shards of broken sky. In the hopes that I may bring, a way to help the pieces heal. So that the stones which coat your bones, will wilt until you feel. That I merely wish to love, what so many have tried to steal. So that when the spin begins to slow, you'll know that I was for real...

CLYDE HURLSTON

My Mistress

Darling, tell me... What if I could penetrate, this shade of your despair? Would it be wise to wait, to pour my love in there? So I could drown your doubt, and turn you inside out. Then wait for the brighter view, that you hid inside of you. 'Cause I won't stop until I find, a way inside your mind. And I will surely paint my face, all across this place. Until you'd begin to burn, and wait for my return. Darling, I pray you yearn for me, until you learn to be... my mistress. Now tell me... What if I could mount your hate, and thrust inside your love? Would you then contemplate, what you should rise above? Or would you lay upon your back, and think of things you lack? As you wrap your legs around, every single inch you've found. Knowing that I won't stop until I find, a way inside your mind. And I surely will paint my face, all across this place. Until you'd then begin to burn, and wait for my return. Darling, I pray you yearn for me, until you learn to see. Oh mistress, when you arrive, will you make me feel alive? And watch these inhibitions die, as I kiss inside your thigh? Oh girl, come and make me beg, for what lies between each leg. And I will use this blessed tongue, to take you up each rung. That Jacob used that day, to get past the skies of gray. And get to that brighter place, that has supplied your grace. So come and let this soul devour, every minute in your hour. And I will show you things, that will make those choirs sing. And they'll remind you, that I won't stop until I find, a way inside your mind. And I will surely paint my face, all across this place. Until you'd then begin to burn, and wait for my return. Darling, yearn for me, until you learn to see... Until you learn to be... Until you live to be... Until you love to be... My mistress. For you may be the one I'd hold, and you may have the thing I crave. But honesty's better when it's told, and tonight, I'll remove your desire from it's grave. And I will cherish everything we do, and our closed doors will concur. That I enjoy tearing into you, as if you truly were... My mistress.

CLYDE HURLSTON

Stiletto Angel

Darling, won't you come down and save me? Or maybe just enslave me. Make me feel like I'm worth affection, and not depression's infection. Then she spread her white wings, and bathed me in her light rings. I seen reflections of my own soul, so now I submit to her control. And I say, "Angel, thank you, for everything you're doing. And stopping my pursuing. My search has finally reached its end. And again I'll thank you, for the lost soul that you're saving. Gave me what I've been craving. Now I'm forever yours my friend." But I wonder, is she really an angel? 'Cause just then things took a dark turn, her wings began a slow burn. And it had a smell that you can notice, but her smile won't let me focus. My heart was yearly yearning, but there's a lesson I wasn't learning. Don't judge a book based on the covers, and don't make strangers your lovers. But still I say, "Angel, thank you, for everything you're doing. And stopping my pursuing. My search has finally reached its end. And again I'll thank you, for the lost soul that you're saving. Gave me what I've been craving. Now I'm forever yours my friend." Oh, she made me smile, if only for awhile. I thought angels had to fly, but she could only fall with style. But still I feel I have a reason to say, "Angel, thank you, for everything you're doing. And stopping my pursuing. My search has finally reached its end. And again I'll thank you, for the lost soul that you're saving. Gave me what I've been craving. Now I'm forever yours my friend." But after all this time I've waited, now I'm completely devastated. To learn that you were not true. But I until I find my other half... I guess you'll just have to do.

A DEBT PAID IN INK

Letter To A Spider

Dear Spider,

Thank you for nothing. Except for one-night of half-hearted pleasure. It was more than I had for the time being. And at the beginning, your sugar-coated lies were too much for even a seasoned fly to resist. Sure I flew to see you once, and candlelight surrounded a satin-covered web. I enjoyed my stay, even as you crawled all over me. Then you took me inside of you, as if it was the only thing you ever wanted to do. More lies were spilled in between your moans. How my words made you cry. And how at night you dreamed of finding a fly like me. And I cant forget your offer to see your scars. As proof, to let my love pour into you. Oh, my darling widow, how sweet they did sound. But make no mistake friend, lying isn't the only thing you do well with your mouth. I would fly to the web one more time, to feel its' talents for old time's sake. But slowly you were losing interest, because I am such a wary fly. So you were slowly turning a cold shoulder towards me. And as the temperatures dropped, your web slowly but surely lost its hold. And with the threat of directing justified words your way, you banished me from the web. And I was ostracized for calling you out on unconfirmed discretions. And oh, how childish the widow can be, when she has lost her hold. It is truly a comical situation. And then I became the inquisitive fly, and offered questions dressed up in apologies to see if I could return to the web. For which I felt a little foolish. But alas, my request was denied. And much to my surprise, and as possible proof of my suspicions, I have come to find you have quickly caught another in your web. But the only change, is that you claim to have given him your heart. Which I find to be pathetically cliché. Unless of course, your new fly was spending nights in your web, while you were convincing me you weren't like all of the other spiders. It's funny, looking back you are so incredibly see-through. But at the time, when you were in front of me, certain parts of you were blinding me to that fact. And my dear widow, please don't mistake this as a bitter journal of our short time together. But rather as my understanding for the manipulative creature that you are. It's simply in your nature. The difference I hope to make, is if your new fly is as naive as I was, then you should simply reveal your true nature to him at the beginning. And maybe your sugar-coated lies will go down as well with him, as you went down on me. Take care of yourself. It's a jungle out there. And with women, excuse me, widows like you, we flies have to keep our wings ready at a moment's notice. Good luck with the catch. I hope that satin web, still feels as good.

Sincerely,
The Seasoned Fly

A DEBT PAID IN INK

North Star

If I was strong enough to hold you up, I'd leave you there amongst the stars. 'Cause even though the nights are cold, girl your light would still be ours. So baby shine down tonight. 'Cause when I'm down, I don't feel alright. But it's you that brings me up. So can I drink what's within your cup? I'd follow you wherever you are, cause it seems like you're my guiding star. Girl, I'd follow you to the ends of the Earth. The clouds couldn't hope to contain, your love that's coming down like rain. Girl, do you know how much you are worth? If I could touch your celestial body, would you let me do what I pleased? Even though these are thoughts ungodly, I wouldn't leave an inch of you teased. So baby shine down tonight. 'Cause when I'm down, I don't feel alright. But it's you that brings me up. So can I drink what's within your cup? I'd follow you wherever you are, cause it seems like you're my guiding star. Girl, I'd follow you to the ends of the Earth. The clouds couldn't hope to contain, your love that's coming down like rain. Girl, do you know how much you are worth? So now just shine! Shine! And show the world you're mine! Girl, would the skies display the signs? That I was on a cloud with those silver lines? Because that's the way you make me feel. And I would plummet and kiss the sun, if you proved that you were the one. That could convince these wounds of mine to heal. 'Cause I'd follow you wherever you are, cause it seems like you're my guiding star. Girl, I'd follow you to the ends of the Earth. The clouds couldn't hope to contain, your love that's coming down like rain. Girl, do you know how much you are worth? So now will you shine? And show the world you're mine? And I'll be yours until the end of time...

Brighter Side Of Day

Did you ever think, that every time you blink? You would take a part of me? Like I was a photograph, that you slowly tore in half? But we've come to find, it was just the heart of me. And so now I stand here broken. Darling, won't you put me together, and love me forever? And then show me the brighter side of day? Because my dreams have been shattered, and the pieces are scattered. So now there's nothing left to say. Tell me, have you ever thought, that everything we've bought? Isn't worth the price we paid? A lesson never learned, and karma has returned. And it's lying in this bed we've made. And it seems that I'm still broken. Darling, won't you put me together, and love me forever? And then show me the brighter side of day? Because my dreams have been shattered, and the pieces are scattered. So now there's nothing left to say. Oh, I gave you everything I am, but you never gave a damn. You just cast me into the wind. You broke the golden rule, and let me play your fool. But I swear it won't happen again. So now I'm screaming: Darling, don't you put me together, or love me forever. 'Cause I've seen what you call the brighter side of day. And what little I'll amount to, is so much better without you. So choose between goodbye and good riddance, and know that's all I have to say...

CLYDE HURLSTON

The Moth And The Flame

If your friends say I am a moth, then these arms are my wings. And I'll invade the sky, to feel the joy it brings. But this flight that I fly, will only help my eyes to see. That here inside the clouds, is not where I should be. 'Cause if I am a moth, then darling, you truly are the flame. And if there's light inside my eyes, then you are the one to blame. So don't question if desire, is the reason I'd die to be here. Because your love is the fire, that I would die to be near. They say the sky's not as blue, when you've viewed it from below. But when you're upon the ground, you don't notice aspects of the show. Like each time the selfish night, stalks the unsuspecting day. But I don't have to worry love, for I know you will light my way. 'Cause if I am a moth, then darling, you truly are the flame. And if there's light inside my eyes, then you are the one to blame. So don't question if desire, is the reason I'd die to be here. Because your love is the fire, that I would die to be near. But if I get too close, my wings would surely melt. But that pain would not compare, to the loneliness I've felt. Each and every day, before you looked my way. So you can turn these wings to ash, but I'd still be here to stay. 'Cause within these flames I feel, I feel so very much alive. And now I finally feel the way, I've been so long denied. So may your friends feel as if they're free, to view or paint me as the worst. But before every morning comes, I'll speak to you as first. Darling, you can have me, and you can take me. But if this is a dream, please don't wake me. 'Cause you can love me, and your flame can burn me. But please, I beg you, to never turn me. No, darling, don't ever turn me loose. 'Cause if I am a moth, then darling, you truly are the flame. And if there's light inside my eyes, then you are the one to blame. So don't question if desire, is the reason I'd die to be here. Because your love is the only fire, that I would die to be near.

CLYDE HURLSTON

Brainstorm

I feel my body tremble, as my resolve begins to break. Emotions start to roll, crushing all within their wake. But the silence that holds you, alive and ever still. Is the reason why these tidal waves, just will never spill. Still I run, still I run, leaving all this damage done. And I see your body move, with the hopes of grabbing eyes. To justify your ugly ways, so you keep on adding lies. To the growing list of crimes, you've committed on this day. When nonsense fell from parted lips, and you dared to look my way. Now you run, now you run, leaving all this damage done. Now I wish to choke your understanding, and slay your ignorance. So when you found what you had lost, you'd see my fingerprints. But your knee deep in stupidity, and neck deep in the waste. That you let your little life become, so you deserve the taste. That lingers in pathetic mouths, like the one you call your own. And I pray I live to see the day, that you wake broken and alone. Then you'll know how I have felt, each time these eyes would blink. And now I'll reveal what you will find, each time this mind would think. You'd see synapses start to scream, and nerves begin to quake. And there wouldn't be an exit near, for your wasted skin to take. So you'd have to choke and understand, that ignorance was slayed. And you got what you deserved, for the foolish games you played. So bathe inside the hatred dear, this brainstorm's at its' end. While you pretend you're innocent, I'll pretend that you were worth it then...

A DEBT PAID IN INK

Break The Bind

On one of many nights alone, I sat in earshot of the phone. And I tried to hide my hope, but I was losing grip upon the rope. That kept me tied to my position, which looked oddly like submission. But then I thought of you, and I knew what I had to do. I had to break the bind, once placed upon a mind. That spent every waking breath, in the slowest form of death. But when wanting more from life, helps you forget about the strife. Then it can't be all that bad, to want what you have never had. Or can it be? 'Cause on one of many nights alone, the same old show was shown. Talking heads that do their best, to make a name just like the rest. But there is nothing they could say, that could take these thoughts away. Because all I ever sought to do, was to get a greater taste of you. But I have to break the bind, once placed upon a mind. That spent every waking breath, in the slowest form of death. But when wanting more from life, helps you forget about the strife. Then it can't be all that bad, to want what you have never had. Or can it be? 'Cause I see your every photograph, and all I can ever do is laugh. Because I still feel like this, sad you don't know that I exist. At least not in any kind of light, that'll place you next to me tonight. So as headphones sing this soul to sleep, I hide the disappointment that I keep. 'Cause I have to break the bind, once placed upon a mind. That spent every waking breath, in the slowest form of death. But when wanting more from life, helps you forget about the strife. Then it can't be all that bad, to want what you have never had. Or can it be? 'Cause girl, I hope the person on your mind proves to be worth your precious time. 'Cause every second that I spent, made it much harder to relent. From my inner child's belief, that you would bring to relief. To the chaos in my heart, before I stopped and fell apart. But now I'll smile... Because I know... Attraction was the bind, I once placed upon my mind. As I spent every waking breath, in the slowest form of death. But when wanting more from life, helps you forget about the strife. Then it can't be all that bad, to want you, since you're what I have never had. Or can you be? Oh, darling for once, can you finally be? No, I think not...

A DEBT PAID IN INK

The Perfect Find

If I could paint a perfect picture, I'm sure the brush would race. To cause this canvas friction, as it made an outline of your face. But since I can't paint worth my weight, I have to write these words for you. 'Cause when I feel this weightless, what else is there to do? But to say those three words, that are often used too much. Since it's what you deserve my love, for you saved me with your touch. But I'll hold those three words back my dear, and wait until the perfect time. Since this lifelong journey has, finally resulted in the perfect find. But after digging deep for so long, I feel my bones they need a rest. Since they proved to be strong enough, to find the heart inside my chest. And I was surprised to find it beating, since it barely made a sound. But the beat did its' best to thunder when, the walls fell and hit the ground. And now I want to say those three words, that are often used too much. Since it's what you deserve my love, for you saved me with your touch. But I'll hold those three words back my dear, and wait until the perfect time. Since this lifelong journey has, finally resulted in the perfect find. And that find was the inner peace, that escaped me in the past. Back when happiness was fleeting fast, and it never seemed to last. And since life would often trick me, and make me out to be naive. So rejection came far too frequently, for I was that easy to deceive. But wrong me once, and you will bear the blame. Do it twice, and it's mine to own. And after I hate what I became, I couldn't stand to be alone. For I built my walls so very well, not a soul could scale the face. Of what was then a monument, of lost faith along with grace. But now I want to say those three words, that are often used too much. Since it's what you deserve my love, for you saved me with your touch. But I'll hold those three words back my dear, and wait until the perfect time. Since this lifelong journey has, finally resulted in the perfect find. Because you seemed to come along, with a timing so divine. That I couldn't believe you'd want me, and I even tried to change your mind. But thankfully I surely failed, to become the fool I tried to play. So now I'll wisely hold on to you, and be damned if I ever let you get away...

A DEBT PAID IN INK

Your Halo

It's when you say those simple things, that I'm inclined to see your wings. But it's often then I know, I'll see the quiet night it brings. But it's when you scream and shout, that I know that I'm about. To close my eyes and feel, as you try to turn me out. So I start to crack a smile, I've been waiting all this time. For you to lose the shine, that hangs above your mind. 'Cause we don't have to be in love, we can just try our hands at lust. Baby, we don't need the world, no, all we need is us. So come and take my hand, since I'm in a mood to play. And know I want to see your horns, but your halo's in the way. And it's when you bite your lip, that i feel my inhibitions slip. And it's when we're working up a sweat, that I fear I'll lose my grip. But then I'd reach out for your hair, and I know you wouldn't care. 'Cause if I could see my back, I'd know your fingernails were there. So I start to crack a smile, I've been waiting all this time. For you to lose the shine, that hangs above your mind. 'Cause we don't have to be in love, we can just try our hands at lust. Baby, we don't need the world, no, all we need is us. So come and take my hand, since I'm in a mood to play. And know I want to see your horns, but your halo's in the way. With every blink and every flash, there's a thrust and there's a crash. There's a sigh, there's a scream, you want it slow, you want it fast. I will do all of the above, baby, at least more than once, maybe. And when we're done you can be modest, but on nights like tonight, I need to feel my goddess. So, go on and grab the sheets, and let the pillows have a kiss. 'Cause there's a spot inside of you, that I don't ever wanna miss. Girl, I want your legs to shake, and feel so good you'll wanna cry. You can call me your mistake, and I won't bother to deny. No, I'll just start to crack a smile, I've been waiting all this time. For you to lose the shine, that hangs above your mind. 'Cause we don't have to be in love, we can just try our hands at lust. Baby, we don't need the world, no, all we need is us. So come and take my hand, since I'm in a mood to play. And know I want to see your horns, but your halo's in the way. Baby, I'm so far from a saint, that I have to be a sinner. And that makes the devil on my shoulder, turn out to be the winner. But baby, I don't care, 'cause I already found the prize. That got Adam and his girl, banished for their lives. And it's the kinda knowledge, that's too potent for a tree. And that's how good you look, when you're on top of me. So baby, climb on top, and I'll tell you when to stop. For it feels like dying when you rise, and feels like Heaven when you drop. Girl, I'd swear to be your martyr, if you started riding harder. As I treat your every tear, like a drop of holy water. Oh, cry for me girl, you can cry out to the world. Hell, you can cry to a god, give either choice a whirl. And baby, that's alright, when you're done we'll just turn out the light. Then you can tell you friends, I was your devil for a night...

Impatience Is A Virtue

On the cusp of dreams, I wait.
Ever impatient. Drowning my sorrows,
in a chalice unseen. Oh, my tongue
has become voracious in its lust.
Waiting, to me, is now akin to torture.
A suffering the silent must endure, If
they are to be rewarded. For haste is
the hallmark of fools. And patience is
the weapon of the masters. Yet here I lay,
Somewhere in the middle of the spectrum.
Counting the seconds, until she is mine
again. I pace back and forth, In a cage
that does not exist, and I hunger. Surely
biding my time, and reenacting her
martyrdom in my mind, at least a
thousand times. For passion has taken
me again. She has no idea what she
does to me. But then again, Her smile
says she knows all too well.

CLYDE HURLSTON

Anchors

I would drive clear across town,
for just a little taste. She would
only need to say the word,
and not a second would waste.
'Cause when someone is in your
veins, all it takes is a little time.
And reason goes out the window,
right along with rhyme.
And I'm proud to say I'm crazy,
always in the mood to play.
This girl slipped her anchors in
my bones, to make sure I never
get away. Mission accomplished,
darling I am yours until the shepherd
lifts the veil. I may be the captain
in my mind, but it's you that puts the
wind inside my sail. So tell me, where
do we go from here?

A DEBT PAID IN INK

My Inner Masochist

It's looking like the kind of night, that I have come to love. Where the warmest of embrace, has become a violent sort of shove. And every shoulder here, grows colder by the breath. So pride then begins to fear, it's impending public death. But girl, I saw you smile, before you locked the door. And you threw away the key, like you've done this all before. But that's alright with me, for I've been expecting this. 'Cause what I'll do tonight, is not a gesture you can miss. So pretend my skin is torn and flayed, and now I have displayed. All the parts of me, that you have once ignored.
And it's on these darkened days, that I have been weighed. And left here bleeding like the fool, that keeps on wanting more. And it's looking like the kind of night, where I won't have to hide. And my inner masochist, won't have to be denied. So girl, pull out your favorite blade, and please make sure it shines. So you can cut me nice and slow, right down these solid lines. 'Cause girl, I saw you smile, before you locked the door. And you threw away the key, like you've done this all before. But that's alright with me, for I've been expecting this. 'Cause what I'll do tonight, is not a gesture you can miss. So pretend my skin is torn and flayed, and now I have displayed. All the parts of me, that you have once ignored. And it's on these darkened days, that I have been weighed. And left here bleeding like the fool, that keeps on wanting more. Girl, there is no amazing grace, for this local shade of wretch. With his darkened point of view, that only some will catch. See, the others just disregard, these statements that I make. But I swear they won't fail to see, each pound of flesh you take.

CLYDE HURLSTON

With the passing of a blade, held so tightly in your hand. That you almost cut yourself, each time your arm would land. But dear, I'm not mad at all, 'cause I got my wish fulfilled. But it's too bad my apathy, would end up getting killed. But indifference never helped, do any single thing. That would get your ass to give, my lonely phone a ring. So now I'm acting out, some foolish fantasy. Full of gestures grandiose, just to be the man you'd see. As merely something more, than your shy and quiet friend. Who could make your body shake, if you'd only let him in. But alas I've failed again, it seems my number's never pulled. We just go 'round and 'round, until the circle's truly full. And I'd be lying if I said, that it didn't hurt a bit. But I guess I'm a glutton for the pain, I've come to you to get. And darling, I've tried my best, to get your eyes to see. But I had to crash and burn, 'cause you're adverse to subtlety. So I had to venture out, to emasculate my hidden fears. In the hope I'd censor doubt, but I'm instead forbidden here. 'Cause you've claimed I've painted you, as the tyrant of my life. When all I've ever said, was that you're a goddess with a knife. Who I will beg to kill the parts of me, that are an unattractive sight. While hoping it's the heart of me, that you'll carry home tonight. But girl, I saw you smile, before you locked the door. And you threw away the key, like you've done this all before. But that's alright with me, for I've been expecting this. 'Cause what I'll do tonight, is not a gesture you can miss. So pretend my skin is torn and flayed, and now I have displayed. All the parts of me, that you have once ignored. And it's on these darkened days, that I have been weighed. And left here bleeding like the fool, that keeps on wanting more. It seems my soul has got a curse, that I will never break. 'Cause I keep failing to receive, while giving everything you'll take. And I believe I'm truly prone, to want the ones who will neglect. The desires, hopes, and dreams, that a small number would collect. But I guess that's life for me, I'll have to live it 'til it's done. And accept I'll never taste the goddess, that will never seem to come...

CLYDE HURLSTON
Fall With Style

If your friends say I'm a jumper love, guess who is my favorite ledge. I'm hoping you'll call my number love, 'cause life is better on the edge. So please don't try to take my hand, just step back and understand. That when my body's flying proper, there's just one place I want to land. So I'll step up and take a dive, until I make you feel alive. As I drift away beneath your waist, finding life's got a better taste. Than it's ever had before, and please believe I'd die for more. So open up and take me in, and I will fall with style again. If your friends say I'm an angel love, guess whose name is on my wings. But this sinner needs a manger love, and it makes me hope you'll say the things. That would often get you dirty looks, from the elders reading out of books. But back when they were half their age, their hands did more than turn a page. And I bet it was the kind of thing, that could stop a churchbell's ring. But now they get to sit and judge, but from this ledge I'll never budge. I'll just step up and take a dive, until I make you feel alive. As I drift away beneath your waist, finding life has got a better taste. Than it's ever had before, and please believe I'd die for more. So open up and take me in, and I will fall with style again. I'm like some kind of phantom love, the need for me's ringing in your brain. It's what you cannot rise above, so just let me kiss away your pain. Put your fingers in my hair love, no, I don't really care who sees us. Show them you're lacking any care love, as your heart and soul cry out for Jesus. Now we're back in the midst of sin, that's what happens when you let me in. And don't deny it feels like home, 'cause the need for this is in your bones. So you lay down and I will take a dive, and girl I'll make you feel alive. As I drift away beneath your waist, finding life has got a better taste. Than it's ever had before, and please believe I'd die for more. So open up and take me in, and I will fall with style again. Oh love, see the look that's in my eyes, every time you make those godly tones. It makes me want to spend my life, braving all these flying stones. Thrown by ones who live inside of glass, hiding from their dark reflection. But my present overshadows pasts, 'cause I get to taste your sweet perfection. So lay your burdens down to rest, after another long and endless day. Place my hands upon your breast, as my tongue comes out to play. And it's these perfect hills he'll roam, until he finds that valley pure. It's over every inch he'll comb, of this fact, my love I'm sure. So you lay down and I will take a dive, and girl I'll make you feel alive. As I drift away beneath your waist, finding life has got a better taste. Than it's ever had before, and please believe I'd die for more. So open up and take me in, then tell your friends I fell with style again...

CLYDE HURLSTON
Living To Please Me

I'll take you and I'll touch you, in any way that I please. And what you've been doing, would bring them to their knees. But not me love, I'm waiting, for proof that you're wet. So I can take my advantage, without a hint of regret. And if you could speak, I know that you would concur. But it's still up to me, how long this will occur. 'Cause ours is a love, they don't understand. And darling I need you, the way you need my hand. So here we go again, relapsing with love. For it's the space between the lines, that we can't rise above. So I'll take you and I'll free you, from this cold-hearted cage. While saints judge us sinners, I'm fast becoming the sage. That will take you and bleed you, all over this place. And the landscape beneath you, will love the way you taste. And if you could speak, I know that you would concur. But it's still up to me, how long this will occur. 'Cause ours is a love, they don't understand. And darling I need you, the way you need my hand. So here we go again, relapsing with love. For it's the space between the lines, that we can't rise above. And I know the others may see you, but not the way that I do. Some have tried their hardest to save you, but when all's said and through. There will be far more of you, than there will be of me. So baby, get back to working, or you'll rest beneath my feet. And if you could see, would there be fear in your eyes. Since it's still up to me, if this love ever dies. 'Cause ours is a love, they don't understand. And darling I need you, the way you need my hand. So here we go again, relapsing with love. For it's the space between the lines, that we can't rise above. And yet a notion has struck me, like a blinding ray of light. That maybe, you're not enjoying, what we're doing here tonight. 'Cause you're not dancing on the surface, so you're fast becoming worthless. And you're refusing to continue, to release what I've put within you. So I'll scream, "Don't go dry, are you trying to tease me? Love, remember your purpose, you're living to please me. So I'll take you and I'll break you, if that's what I choose. For you're not the one I will marry, but just the one that I'll use. 'Cause you're just an ink pen, that I found in my drawer. And my hands felt so good, you came back for more. But now you're not writing, so you're no good to me. And now I'll uncap another, to show you how true love should be. So while you're placed in the trash, I'm sure you may regret me. But I beg you to tell them, that they will never forget me. And darling, neither will you!"

CLYDE HURLSTON
The Greatest Gift To Man

It's so hard in modern days, for the greatest gift to man. That they claim we help to form, when He placed a rib on chosen land. And then we saw her take shape, in these tales of yester year. But now friend, they've left us, with discontent to fester here. She'll face assaults from magazines, and whispers from the crowds. While phony friends and articles, just aim their armor-piercing rounds. Hoping to tear her godly skin, with the words they hold within. But these fools will never understand, girl, you're the greatest gift to man. And through mistakes you may have made, they stole the shine from off your blade. But darling, I will make a point of you, by sharpening your point of view. Into a force of will alone, strong as steel and light as bone. That's wielded by a soul in pain, who won't be victimized again. And it's so hard in modern days, to see through ancient ignorance. 'Cause if you looked at all our lives, you'd see a woman's fingerprints. They helped shape us and guide us, when we were lost in seas of pride. And if I've felt closer to Heaven, with each girl I've been inside. But sometimes I'll admit, anger outweighs the things I feel. But that doesn't mean my love, for all women isn't real. It's just that sometimes I worry, that I'll be alone on dying days. So I'm sorry if I'm in a hurry, to bury ancient man's dying ways. 'Cause those fools will never understand, a woman is the greatest gift to man. And through mistakes you may have made, they stole the shine from off your blade. But darling, I will make a point of you, by sharpening your point of view. Into a force of will alone, strong as steel and light as bone. That's wielded by a soul in pain, who won't be victimized again. And it's so hard in darkened days, to even find a hint of light. But I can think of all the ways, your smile will help me see tonight. That I'm both blessed and chosen, to be here at your side. As you melt a heart once frozen, after the years it was denied. Any semblance of a channel, in which to flow so very free. And I can't help but to feel, there's no place I'd rather be. Than beneath these bright stars, with my head inside your lap. 'Cause I finally understand, girl, you're greatest gift to man. And through mistakes you may have made, they stole the shine from off your blade. But darling, I will make a point of you, by sharpening your point of view. Into a force of will alone, strong as steel and light as bone. That's wielded by a soul in pain, who won't be victimized again. And when you stand with shoulders squared, as the wind plays inside your hair. I want you to remember certain things, like how love may hurt and sting. But just because that statement's true, it shouldn't mean the world to you. For you have too much inner light to dim, and it's just the gift you got from Him. And I'm also witness to your modesty, but you're a goddess honestly. So you should not forget, that there are things you may regret. And while they've forgotten what you're worth is, darling, it does not make you worthless. So with your actions of true grace, use the smile that's on your face. To make these fools understand, a woman is the greatest gift to man...

CLYDE HURLSTON

ACT II:
POP CULTURE CRUCIFIXION

A DEBT PAID IN INK

Speak Softly

Baby, what I need from you, is a little, "here and now". 'Cause you speak of yesterdays, and I hear you wonder how. Your phone has fallen silent, and nobody wants to ring. So you grab your blackened book, to start recalling everything. First you try the blonds, and then you try the reds. Then you convince yourself, you prefer brunettes instead. But we both know the truth, I see the desperate in your eyes. Then you come over to impress me, by telling all your lies. As you start leaning in, to whisper in my ear. Trying to figure out the things, that I may want to hear. But what you fail to see, is I'm not fond of tales. And it's when a man speaks softly, that his bigger stick prevails. And now what I get from you, is a little, "how it was". As you speak of yesterdays, since nobody ever does. Oh, but I'm not interested, in anything but truth. And I think immaturity, is an insult to our youth. So you better try the blonds, and then you can try the reds. As you convince yourself, you prefer brunettes instead. But we both know the truth, I see the desperate in your eyes. So friend, you can't impress me, by telling all your lies. And as you start leaning in, to whisper in my ear. Trying to figure out the things, that I may want to hear. But what you fail to see, is I'm not fond of tales. And it's when a man speaks softly, that his bigger stick prevails. Oh, I see you walking tall, and that's alright with me. But you've let your pride become, an imagined right to be. Here all up in my face, hiding horns behind a grin. And claiming that my place, is where you should be in. But honey, I don't roll that way, I don't know you from the wall. And my heels are dug in deep, to make sure I'll never fall. For the tired sort of tricks, you've pulled out from your bag. And keep what's up your sleeve, that's left you so inclined to brag. About bedding all the blonds, and leaving all the reds. As you convince yourself, you prefer brunettes instead. But we both know the truth, I see the desperate in your eyes. So friend, you can't impress me, by telling all your lies. As you start leaning in, to whisper in my ear. Trying to figure out the things, that I may want to hear. But what you fail to see, is I'm not fond of tales. And it's when a man speaks softly, that his bigger stick prevails. See, the owner of the magic stick, should never have to boast. Unless he's really insecure, then he's sure to talk the most. And then he'll overcompensate, with sharp clothes and shiny things. Thinking he can buy my heart, and own the body that it brings. But that will never happen, in this life or the next. 'Cause I won't be the latest notch, that belt of his collects. So you go back to your blonds, or crawl back to the reds. Or stay here and buy a drink, for those brunettes instead. But we both know the truth, I see the desperate in your eyes. So friend, you can't impress me, by telling all your lies. So please don't bother leaning in, to whisper in my ear. Since you'll never figure out the things, that I may want to hear. 'Cause the signs you failed to read, or even understand. Are gonna send you home tonight, and help that stick to meet your hand...

Rise & Fall

Shall we roll that carpet out, and make it start to bleed? Since you have a reputation, that you have to feed. So we'll put your name in lights, until it starts to burn. And hope it doesn't turn to ash, until you've had your turn. But the brightest stars are burning out, and now the world is turning out. There's not a soul who won't recall, the day that you began to fall... But we can roll that carpet out, and help you see the red. So you can find the quickest way, to be the next up and comer dead. Then you can snort your lines, as the records start to climb. Then we'll etch you on the list, of those who left here in their prime. But the brightest stars are burning out, and now the world is turning out. There's not a soul who won't recall, the day that you began to fall. And as you start to take a dive, you'll help these fools to feel alive. And I will sit and shake my head, while reciting words that I once said. So roll that carpet out, and make it start to bleed. Since I've got that good advice, that you refuse to heed... As your knees begin to buckle, and your shoulders start to bruise. It's your expensive grip, that you can't afford to lose. Or else the world will tumble, off that back you own. And those who watched you rise, will watch you fall alone. Because they know... The brightest stars are burning out, and now the world is turning out. There's not a soul who won't recall, the day that you began to fall. And as you start to take a dive, you'll help these fools to feel alive. And I will sit and shake my head, while reciting words that I once said...

Monumental

Very few people will place their hands in the dirt, and help you build your foundation. Most will just want to visit your creation when it is completed. And others have declared it monumental. Then, they will come in droves, to take their pictures there. Just to prove they witnessed your greatness firsthand. Where were they in the beginning? How did they aid in your struggle? Or was it when your name invaded households far and wide, did they come to call you friend with pride? How can you trust those that never saw you, until your name was in the lights?

Timing & Lighting

The star that burns twice as
bright often burns for half as long,
but when you illuminate their night
they'll never say you're wrong.
So make your ridiculous demands,
then go print them on a list
that your assistant will provide,
while you deny that it exists.
Then you can tell the press
they misconstrue your words,
and they're stingy with the praise
your precious work deserves.
But they'll tolerate your every whim
if you're sure to fill the seats,
or if you give them crazy tales
to print boldly on their sheets.
Tell me what's the good of shining
if no one's there to see, and
what's the good of timing
if you have no where to be?
Oh, what's the good of learning
if you don't practice what you teach,
and what's the good of earning
if your dreams are not in reach?

CLYDE HURLSTON
Go For The Gold

That brighter shade of bronze, is what nobody wants. And nobody's showing off, 'cause nobody ever taunts. Unless they're on the top, unless they've never dropped. And only chased the finish line, when they heard the pistol pop. But who are you to say, you know the only way? That I should stop and roll, just to push the flames away. Should I hold my tongue, 'til Jacob's fabled rung. Replaced the mighty edge, from which I might've hung. You're better than everyone, just because you know the son. Who might not've even lived beneath the sun. But I know your little goal, is to save my little soul. So you'll never stop until you get the gold. But when the meek and meager meet, and rest their weary feet. Will paradise ever feel as sugar sweet? As it did to burst your bubble love, when you knelt and looked above. And saw the vultures killing off all the doves. Now it seems the silver spoon, is good for second place. But when inside of greedy mouths, it tends to leave a bitter taste. And behind imported doors, you'll make room for more. Too much is not enough, go purchase more I do implore. Buy lots of pretty things, have fingers draped in rings. While underneath their breath, I hear your servants start to sing. There's gonna come a day, when karma rings the bell. And your house of cards, will have kissed the wind and finally fell. Since you're better than everyone, because you think you've won. Every game we've played beneath the sun. But I know your little goal, is to fill the growing hole. That will never stop until you get the gold. But when the meek and meager meet, and rest their weary feet. Paradise will never feel as sugar sweet. As it did to burst your bubble love, when you knelt and looked above. And saw the vultures killing off all the doves. Then you finally realized, that you were the biggest vulture of them all.

CLYDE HURLSTON

(LUCKY SPERM CLUB)

There's a brand new set of rules, that some are bound to use. And when families come from wealth, they don't have to pay their dues. They just pass the velvet rope, dropping names into the air. And whoever holds the little list, will find these souls on there. It's not who you are but what you wear, and tabloids are what you must bear. To keep yourself in public eyes, since Larry King will hear your cries. And this is how it feels to be, a member of the L.S.C.. So you can ask for autographs, but all you're bound to get are laughs. Both the Hilton girls were superstars, so many people know their name. The Jenner girls are cashing in, and there's a few Kardashians to blame. But the johnny's coming lately will, steal their shine away. And since nobody's heard of me, who cares what I have to say? When it's not who you are but what you wear, the tabloids are a pain that you must bear. To keep yourself in public eyes, since People magazine will print your cries. And this is how it feels to be, a member of the L.S.C.. Naked selfies are worth their weight in gold, if you've already sold your soul. I walk with my nose in the sky, and only bring it down to get me high. I cram that powder in my nose, and starve to fit designer clothes. You can't resist my smile and charm, or see the holes inside my arm. Place the pills on top my tongue, while botox keeps my face so young. 'Cause it's not who you are but what you wear. And paparazzi are what you must bear. To keep yourself in public eyes, just let TMZ record your cries. 'Cause this is how it feels to be, a member of the L.S.C.. And when reality becomes far too much, we'll give you ways to lose your touch.

A DEBT PAID IN INK

Ctrl + Alt + Del

I often have wandered down paths that I've tread. All without any thinking, just scratching my head. I moved in any direction, with a lack of discretion. Now I'm so lost and uncertain, with so much to question. But no answers are given, to someone like me. So cold and ungrateful, for all that I see. But then I start praying, when I'm in a mess. All while hiding my wish, for someone to press. Control, alt, delete, since I'm so incomplete. And I'm dying for bliss, and my soul to meet. I've been down on my knees, before finding my feet. But I'm still prone to thinking, "My pain's on repeat." So will you forgive me, for things that I've done? And halt this train of thought, that I couldn't outrun. For I'm the conductor, with full steam ahead. And it's just a matter of time, before I end up dead. But that will be something, for someone who cares. Like those failing to see, my beautiful flares. That have burned on the nights, when I reached a low. Because a burning self-hatred, just continued to glow. But help isn't given, to someone like me. So cold and ungrateful, for all that I see. But then I start praying, when I'm in a mess. All while hiding my wish, for someone to press. Control, alt, delete, since I'm so incomplete. And I'm dying for bliss, and my soul to meet. I've been down on my knees, before finding my feet. But I'm still prone to thinking, "My pain's on repeat." Oh, Lord, if I had a dime, for each fucking time. That I've ever failed, I could build me a shrine. But after each bill would fold, I'd have nothing to hold. Because I'm just a fool, undeserving of gold. So someone tell the rich, they'll never worry in the least. Because I will never own, anything above a lease.

Since this working life of mine, has only made me a slave. Leave me to the water I tread, And I'll break in each wave. Because nothing is given, to someone like me. So cold and ungrateful, for all that I see. But then I start praying, when I'm in a mess. All while hiding my wish, for someone to press. Control, alt, delete, since I'm so incomplete. And I'm dying for bliss, and my soul to meet. I've been down on my knees, before finding my feet. But I'm still prone to thinking, "My pain's on repeat." And the world's still in motion, so I have a notion. That your expectations, are still vast like an ocean. But would you rather see, me drowned in that sea? Or with a penny for the one, that's burned in effigy? 'Cause fate isn't kind, to someone like me. Who's cold and ungrateful, for all that I see. But then I start praying, when I'm in a mess. All while hiding my wish, for someone to press. Control, alt, delete, since I'm so incomplete. And I'm dying for bliss, and my soul to meet. I've been down on my knees, before finding my feet. But I'm still prone to thinking, "My pain's on repeat." And why can't you see, that I'm such a mess? And if there is a God, you'll be a good friend and press. Control, alt, delete, fuck I'm so incomplete. And I'm dying for bliss, to take hold within. I've been down on my knees, before finding my feet. But I'm still prone to screaming, "Will this... ever... end?!"

A DEBT PAID IN INK

Hey Little Junkie

Come in little junkie, start closing the door. I can tell by your eyes, that you're dying for more. I know you had a want, that's fast becoming a need. So now you come to daddy, just hoping he'll feed. The gaping hole in your soul, that's finally been exposed. So it's hard to hide the truth about your legs, since they won't stay closed. And that's just fine with me, because I'm just dying to see. If you'll tell your friends, how much higher you'll be. 'Cause first you were the girl, that wouldn't get high. But now you're leaving this world, and you're hoping to fly. Well, just blame it on me, since I'm a hell of a guy. But know I'm not the one, who said to give it a try. So, hey little junkie, let's start trying your luck. So you can scream to the world, if you're dying to fuck. 'Cause you're always gonna beg, for one more round. Knowing that once I'm inside, you ain't ever comin' down. Come on little junkie, are you feelin' my charms? If so, start by tying this belt, around one of your arms. Yeah, get it nice and tight, now let's find your vein. Then I'll kiss your lips, so you won't mind your pain. Then I'll slide it in, and you'll start to grin. 'Cause you got your fix, for free right here again. But then you start to pout, as I'm slowly pulling out. But I'll go in again, oh baby, don't have a doubt. Yet every time I hold you close, I worry that you'll overdose. 'Cause first you were the girl, that wouldn't get high. Now you're leaving the world, and hoping to fly. Well, you can blame it on me, 'cause I'm a hell of a guy. But know I'm not the one, who said to give it a try. So, hey little junkie , let's start trying your luck. So you can scream to the world, if you're dying to fuck. 'Cause you're always gonna beg, for one more round. Knowing that once I'm inside, you ain't ever comin' down...

CLYDE HURLSTON

Food For Your Syringe

To navigate the upper class, we'll see just how low you'll go. But seconds here will briefly pass, so it's your best that you must show. Paint your face and gloss your lips, don't forget to show some skin. Now touch your dreams with fingertips, you'll never get this close again. The junkies have begun to binge, on the food in their syringe. So take the belt and tie it tight, and you may see the stars tonight. But if your life's begun to hinge, on the food in your syringe. Then you'll either overdose, or spend your life still comatose. Ingest the lines with open eyes, since they're all that we can see. Place your bibles out of view, then tune in to TMZ. 'Cause the fumes of the rumors, will stoke sense of humors. But I'll be here and laughing last, as you try to hide your past. The junkies have begun to binge, on the food in their syringe. So take the belt and tie it tight, and you may see the stars tonight. But if your life's begun to hinge, on the food in your syringe. Then you'll either overdose, or spend your life still comatose. You're washing up on Jersey Shore, or making mountaintops of Hills. But I'm beyond caring less, with the lengths you'll go for thrills. So feed your needs until you bleed, but I won't dare clean up your mess. And as your eyes roll into your head, I'll hope you enjoy that view the best. Cause you say real life is not as fun, as this fantasy has become. But to me you've lost your mind, or your eyes have fallen blind. So stay away from me and mine, I don't care to waste the time. That it would take to wake you up, and my tolerance is breaking up. Since the junkies have begun to binge, on the food in their syringe. So take the belt and tie it tight, and you may see the stars tonight. But if your life's begun to hinge, on the food in your syringe. Then you'll either overdose, or spend your life still comatose...

CLYDE HURLSTON

The Gift That You Give

Dancing through the tops of the trees, was the slightest of breeze. That would carry a soul, but could not make it whole. For that was the task, of a God so divine. That He ruled the world, since the dawn of our time. But as I look to the sky. I ask, "are the stories a lie?" 'Cause faith is a gift, I have yet to receive. But there are some things, I'm inclined to believe. Like the way that you move, is proof that you can. Just do what you do, and make me feel like a man. Dancing on the darkest of floors, was a goddess in view. And the club lights would shine, 'til the sky turned to blue. But since we owned the night, I told the morning to stay. So sound asleep, that the darkness could play. But as I looked in her eyes, I saw a hint of the prize. And yet still faith is a gift, I have yet to receive. But there are some things, I'm inclined to believe. Like the way that you move, is proof that you can. Just do what you do, and make me feel like a man. Girl there are some things, that I need to confess. Before this encounter of ours, oh, my life was a mess. That could not be cleaned, or be organized. Because it was myself, that I so greatly despised. Because faith was a gift, I had yet to receive. But there were some things, I was inclined to believe. Like the way that I was, brought disaster around. But all it took was your touch, to put my feet on the ground. And this gift that you give, could help me to live. For more than a day, and throw my burdens away. But there comes a time, when they're bound to return. Then I'll come to find, there's still lessons to learn. But until we reach that day, all that I'll ask of you. Is to please never stop, doing that thing that you do...

A DEBT PAID IN INK

Consequence Of Pop

Baby, everybody loves you here, you're never turned away. But let me make this crystal clear, when it's your turn to play. There'll be no limits left to reach, when the world is yours to own. And the lessons that this life'll teach, won't help when you're alone. So once we roll that carpet out, and make it start to bleed. You will have a reputation that, you will have to feed. And we'll put your name in the lights, until it starts to burn. And hope it doesn't turn to ash, until you've had your turn. If you're the one who gets the fame, may your fortune never stop. And you never have the press to blame, for the consequence of pop. And I hope your star burns as bright, as it did on yesterday. 'Cause you'll forget the sound of no, when you say yes and press play. Baby, everybody wants you here, since you're such a pretty face. There's not a thing for you to fear, so just take another taste. I'll draw the lines for you to see, until you find out the smell. As everything you ever dreamed, becomes the tale you'll tell. But we'll still roll that carpet out, and help you see the red. So you can find the quickest way, to be the one they found dead. As you snort the lines I drew, your records start their climb. Then we'll etch your name upon the list, of those who left in their prime. If you're the one who gets the fame, may your fortune never stop. And you never have the press to blame, for the consequence of pop. Hope your star burns as bright, as it did on yesterday. 'Cause you'll forget the sound of no, when you say yes and press play. Baby, everybody flaunts it here, whether confidence or swag. And you're name's not as important, as the name on your bag. And leave the tags upon the rags, that hide your chiseled frame. 'Cause when it all hangs out for us to see, you'll have the internet to blame.

A DEBT PAID IN INK

The Lies That Bind

If all the world's a stage, then we're performers in a sense. And the characters we play, are just our last defense. For we feel we must protect, the things so near and dear. That it's the truth we will neglect, so our lies can bind us here. But look at you my darling star, you seem to shine as bright. As the other stars seem to glow, inside my sky at night. But since we're placed upon this stage, my attention rarely goes. Anywhere that you are not, and I hope, no better yet I suppose. That you have something to do, with this one-track line of thought. That runs throughout my nightly dreams, since sleep has surely brought. Here to me a better way, of exploring your temple walls. And my wants become these blooming needs, each time your temple calls. And then the silence begins to grow, the three words you wished to hear. And as this truth begins to show, I whisper them softly in your ear. And as you take each one to heart, I follow the path I took before. Far beyond those tempting gates, I once referenced out of lore. But this character I play today, has no love for stories told. He merely wants to just explore, so his warmth will mask the cold. Then the darling star awoke to shine, and found the sky was not as filled. As it was the night before, and so her tears were spilled. For she felt the script that he had used, made a mockery of rules. And all his excavation proved, was that love was only for fools. That forget we are upon a stage, and no soul can prove it wrong. So put on your mask and hide yourself, for here we all belong...

The Pulpit & The Runway

Yeah, baby strut your stuff, walk with a purpose for me please. Show me the latest of the threads, as you give my eyes a tease. Sell myself some confidence, with the way you sharply turn. Prove that thin is the only form, in which the fires hotly burn. Let the public get a taste, for beauty as it's sold. Since they can pay the steepest price, and have it be theirs to hold. For the brand is more important, than life or self-respect. So be sure to tell your designer, about the praise that you collect. Oh, the pulpit and the runway, are places so divine. The shepherds show their face, and the sheep will form a line. But did we ever stop to think, about the fact we have to pay. For getting judged by the ones, who'll take our souls away. Yeah, Father preach the word, until you teach us all of sin. Tell us of the One, who caused this world to begin. Then you can tell us of the light, as the collection plate is passed around. Then threaten us with torture, in the fires below the ground. Oh, the pulpit and the runway, are places so divine. The shepherds show their face, and the sheep will form a line. But did we ever stop to think, about the fact we have to pay. For getting judged by the ones, who'll take our souls away. Whether for a moment, or for eternity...

A DEBT PAID IN INK

The Devil Wears A Dress

Inside some hole in the wall, I'm neck deep inside a mess. 'Cause I mistook an angel, for the devil that's in a dress. So tight it could suffocate, and it's hotter than the devil's skin. Lord, I tried to look away, but I just had to look again. Once said I wanted to see her horns, but forgot a rose has got her thorns. So now her poison is in my vein, and I'm losing her favorite game. Oh, my friend you will not believe, I'm an Adam without an Eve. 'Cause Lilith is in my view, so what is a man to do? Should I just turn and run, and hope that night is done? Knowing I'll never near the door, 'cause I got what I'm asking for. There's evil inside her smile, I detect it beneath her lips. Now lipstick is on the glass, from which she slowly sips. And she's locking her eyes on me, I'm like a young deer in lights. So it's really not hard to see, how I'm spending my lonely nights. Said I wanted to see her horns, but forgot a rose has got her thorns. So now her poison is in my vein, and I'm losing her favorite game. Oh, my friend you will not believe, I'm an Adam without an Eve. 'Cause Lilith is in my view, so what is a man to do? Should I just turn and run, and hope that night is done? Knowing I'll never near the door, 'cause I got what I'm asking for. You must be careful with a wish, for it can never be withdrawn. And while searching for a queen, I've moved squarely as a pawn. And for a woman such as her, the chase is now the king. So everything I'd like to do, will never mean a thing. 'Cause to her a compliment, is just a sugar-coated bore. So now my knees are making love, to this god-forsaken floor. And I'm looking up at her, wondering what is in my drink. While the world is turning gray, just as fast as I can blink. Then she whispers in my ear, five words and then a kiss. And her words were ringing clear, "Baby, you couldn't handle this." Said I wanted to see her horns, but forgot a rose has got her thorns. So now her poison is in my vein, and I'm losing her favorite game. Oh, my friend you will not believe, I'm an Adam without an Eve. 'Cause Lilith is in my view, so what is a man to do? Should I just turn and run, and hope that night is done? Knowing I'll never near the door, 'cause I got what I'm asking for. Her dress was more red than the blood, spilled from many broken hearts. That she left in her wake, after she tore their worlds apart. And I'm just the latest fool, who thought he was the best. But it's here I lay in love, in a pile of pieces like the rest. So if you see her run, don't be tempted by the smile. 'Cause it will spark your pride, and just inflate your guile. And if you touch her skin, you won't be seen again. Unless it's in the Hell, the rest of us are living in...

A DEBT PAID IN INK

Famous Crush

In a fevered rush I hit the room, with a curiosity in bloom. Thinking that I will find a way, to make one of them mine today. Playing out my fantasies, proving that we were meant to be. United here and deep in love, with a constant high to stay above. Ooh baby, it's such a rush. To look and see my famous crush. On silver screens and magazines. And late at night in dirty dreams. Yeah baby, it's such a rush, to look and see my famous crush. On silver screens and magazines, and in my x-rated fantasies. The first stop for me my friend is, the home of Miss Eva Mendes. But do you know the lengths I'd go, to get a kiss from Scarlett Jo? Oh, I would spend more than half a day, in the bed of Anne Hathaway. And I would get down upon my knees, if I could taste my sweet Charlize. And Amber would see me at her door, but I hear she don't like boys no more. So instead I'll go to Britney's place, and spend some time below her waist. Then after she would set me free, I would love to see Miss Cameron D. But if I could be inside Miss Biel, it would mean that God was real. Because I'm having such a rush, when I look and see my famous crush. Here inside this bed with me, lying as still as they can be. Yeah baby, it's such a rush, to look and see my famous crush. On these walls surrounding me, and loving what they've found in me. Oh, maybe Gaga is the one I need, 'cause I have an ego that I've got to feed. And this a warning she should really heed, her poker face is what I'd die to read. I wish my girl was more like Nicole, 'cause it'd be then I could lose control. And tear through designer clothes, I love

Kelly C. and don't care who knows. And every time I blink I start to think, I've got more than a thing for Pink. But Lord I guess that girl was right, 'cause it's just me and my hand tonight. I dream so much I cannot rest, in my mind I'm making love to Zoe S. And how I dream that I can be the one, to make all of these pretty women cum. 'Cause I know it will be such a rush, for them to be inside this bed with me. While tied up, and lying as still as they can be. Yeah baby, it's such a rush, to look and see my famous crush. On all these walls surrounding me, and finally loving what they found in me..."

A DEBT PAID IN INK

How Far I'll Go

I have seen your every film, and heard your every song. And it's in these tired eyes, that you can do no wrong. So won't you flash a smile at me, and sign my every page. Since you've become the star, that lives upon my beating stage. Darling, look how far you've come, and now you're number one. On everybody's list, so why do you resist. The love I wish to give, so I'll find out where you live. And then you'll finally know, just how far I'll go. So I bought myself a map of stars, and found my way to you. And it's through these iron bars, that your temple lies in view. And as I scale the gates, your voice it softly calls. But you are unaware, that I'm roaming through your halls. And I see how far you've come, now that you're number one. On everybody's list, so darling, why do you resist? The love I wish to give, so I had to find out where you live. And now you'll finally know, just how far I'll go. After looking through your drawers, I softly kiss your sheets. Because they get to hold, your body as it sleeps. And then I hear your steps, as soft as they can be. So I start to laugh, because you now belong to me. These shadows hold me tight, here inside your room tonight. And I can see you're barely dressed, and so very far from stressed. And so I jump out from the dark, since you've ignored my bark. And with my hand over your mouth, I think you can finally hear me out. Since I've seen how far you've come, now that you're number one. On my victim list, 'cause you chose to resist. The love I wished to give, so I found out where you live. And now you'll finally know, just how far I'll go...

CLYDE HURLSTON

Commitment Of A Different Sort

In the grips of loneliness, is where I spend my days. I keep losing track of time, so I can't count the ways. I've gave myself excuses, to try and hear your voice. But then these orderlies, came and took away my choice. So now my want's become a need, is what my therapist will say. But they always take your side, when you wear your shirt that way. And the bit of skin you flash, is what got me in this mess. So I'm face down on the ground, with my arms around my chest. And I'm singing... Girl, if I'm single any longer, I will have to be committed. And if your jacket's straight, I'm quite sure I would fit it. So please don't be surprised, when I climb those padded walls. 'Cause you're the one to blame, who won't return my calls. Oh baby, tell me why, do you look so damn confused? When you know that I'm the soul, you've once again refused. And I've longed for you so long, that I just can't find my way. Back to this so-called reality, so on the brink is where I stay. 'Cause my want's become a need, is what the therapist will say. But he'll always take your side, when you wear your shirt that way. And the bit of skin you flash, is what got me in this mess. So I'm face down on the ground, with my arms around my chest. And I'm singing... Girl, if I'm single any longer, I will have to be committed. And if your jacket's straight, I'm quite sure I would fit it. So please don't be surprised, when I climb those padded walls. 'Cause you're the one to blame, who won't return my calls. Here the walls are very soft, and it reminds of your skin. But you're nowhere to be found, and the walls are closing in. But you don't give a shit, 'cause they got me out your hair. So now your phone won't ring, and I won't show up everywhere. But baby you've forgot, how determined I can be. I'll play normal for awhile, until they come and let me free. Then once I hit the streets, I will gladly walk for miles. Until I'm square inside your view, and I see the look that's in your eyes. 'Cause my want is still a need, so I guess the therapist was right. But they always took your side, 'cause you wore your shirt so tight. And the bit of skin you flash, was my favorite memory. And now we can do our best to change, what you said would never be. While I'm singing... Girl, if I'm single any longer, I will have to be committed. And if your jacket's straight, I'm quite sure I would fit it. But I would rather fit your arms, around me for awhile. And I would fight those orderlies, just to see you when you smile. So please don't be surprised, that these words are metaphors. 'Cause you're the one I want, and the one I'll love forevermore. So now when I climb the walls, I will do it just for sport. 'Cause I'll have you in my life, to make a commitment of a different sort...

CLYDE HURLSTON
Medicine In The Candy

If something sounds too good, it's bound to catch your ear. But it's the content placed within, that'll cause you all to fear. So I watch you turn away, or turn the volume down. But I think I've found a way, to turn this thing around. I'll take a candy-coated shell, that's bound to taste so well. That you'll die to have a taste, and lay your fears to waste. And once it's past your lips, then the information slips. Deep inside your mind, to enhance your life in time. And if something looks too good, it's bound to catch your eyes. And if it's in designer rags, you'll treat it like a prize. 'Cause you won't dig beneath, the layers that you see. With the hopes of finding out, how deep this well could be. So I'll take a candy-coated shell, that's bound to taste so well. That you'll die to have a taste, and lay your fears to waste. And once it's past your lips, then the information slips. Deep inside your mind, to enhance your life in time. And you don't realize, that you've let us in. Because the flavor often hides, the taste of medicine. Friend, are you afraid I'll preach, or just afraid I'll teach? How to look beyond, the flashing box that's always on. Draining every drop of sense, from those upon the fence. Gazing at the other side, with greener grass they've been denied. Forcing me to take a candy-coated shell, that's bound to taste so well. That you'll die to have a taste, and lay your fears to waste. And once it's past your lips, then the information slips. Deep inside your mind, to enhance your life in time. And you don't realize, that you've let us in. Because the flavor often hides, the taste of medicine...

Satellites

The data's on the racks, inside your local store. They beam the pictures down, while we beg them all for more. They show us all the stars, and the shit we love to see. As we get a glimpse at all the things, we know we'll never be. So in case you haven't heard, a picture's worth a thousand words. But it's when they're up for sale, that the checks come in the mail. So don't try to hide your eyes, just start digesting all the lies. We'll put the satellites in flight, you just make sure the price is right. 'Cause when you can buy the world, you don't have a place to hide. But you can do an interview, where all things will get denied. But true colors tend to show, when you're stepping out the car. And your lack of inhibitions will, tend to get you very far. 'Cause the consumers of the rumors, say the dirt is in demand. The suppliers stoke the fires, but nobody understands. The star that shines twice as bright, only burns for half as long. So do what you feel is right, and we won't think it's wrong. At least not at first... And that's because the consumers of the rumors, say the dirt is in demand. The suppliers stoke the fires, still nobody understands. The star that shines twice as bright, only burns for half as long. So do what you feel is right, and we won't think it's wrong. At least not at first. But eventually we'll build you up to tear you down!

CLYDE HURLSTON

The Littlest Of Lies

While lying in a bed, that's motionless and still. Memories choke the mind, and the eyes begin to fill. But the lips are dry and cracked, the surest signs of apathy. And the only one I've loved, is growing mad at me. 'Cause it seems she's heard the news, and she thinks it to be true. And while I didn't light the fuse, I know what she is gonna do. 'Cause it's the littlest of lies, that often compromise. By sparking up the fight, that I'm caught inside tonight. And though the lie was white, her eyes are turning red. And she's screaming back at me, with every word I've said. Now we're standing in the hall, and each has chose an end. Better times still drape the wall, but tonight's too far from then. And as the volume starts to rise, the lights have every right to burn. While causing me to sweat, as the night takes another turn. 'Cause it seems she's heard the news, and she thinks it to be true. And while I didn't light the fuse, I know what she is gonna do. 'Cause it's the littlest of lies, that often compromise. By sparking up the fight, that I'm caught inside tonight. And though the lie was white, her eyes are turning red. And she's screaming back at me, with every word I've said. Now I'm trying to gather up the nerve, to look her in the eyes. And give the truth that she deserves, but I've told so many lies. That she never will believe, that I'm innocent of this. 'Cause when you've always been deceived, the mark gets harder to miss. But I feel I must defend, what little soul remains. But I watch her cross her arms, as I'm trying to explain. That when you're the envy of the town, they will try to bring you down. And the birds will often sing, when they see you wear the ring. But the days that you're alone, no one's calling on the phone. 'Cause they will ever chase the one, who's not bothering to run. And when they see you smile at me, their stomachs start to turn. 'Cause we have the happiness, for which they've yearly yearned. But now your love has turned to hate, as you accuse me of the crimes. That I never would commit, at least, most of the times. But I freely admit my mistakes, while knowing they're paid for in full. But darling, I will never forget, what you're now trying to pull. When you claimed you heard the news, and thought it to be true. Knowing I didn't light the fuse, but you did what you wanted to do. And yes, it's the littlest of lies, that will often compromise. By sparking up the fight, that we're caught inside tonight. And though the lie was white, her red eyes have faded for now. And she's just staring at me, as I kneel down to lift the broken picture of us, that's lying on the ground...

CLYDE HURLSTON

The Circle That You Keep

Friend, I see the circle that you keep. And what you've sown they're sure to reap. And I don't wish this fate for you, but deep down, you know it's true. That the star that burns as bright as yours, only burns for half as long. And when that star begins to fade, the stench of death becomes too strong. For a nose to dare resist, even one as trained as this. But they'll shower you with love, as they swoop down from above. Friend, I see the circle that you keep. And what you've sown they're sure to reap. And I don't wish this fate for you. But deep down, you know it's true. 'Cause the star that shines to light the way, will fade eventually one day. But they build you up to tear your down, here in this sadistic, little town. So when the front page starts to turn, and your bridges start to burn. I hope the fire keeps your warm, 'cause dark skies may just bring you harm. 'Cause I see the circle that you keep, and what you've sown they're sure to reap. And I don't wish this fate for you. But deep down, you know it's true. That the vultures pop up overhead, anytime somebody's dead. And they're here to pick the bones, they'll get rich quick and build their homes. As a darkened circle fills the sky, the way that tears would fill the eye. But these aren't clouds that start to form, it's a sight that's become the norm. In a world obsessed with fame, they see death as a chance to claim. The bit of shine that they can have, as they take what they can grab. So don't let them take you under. 'Cause I see the circle that you keep, and what you've sown they're sure to reap. And I don't wish this fate for you, but deep down, you know it's true. That the vultures pop

A DEBT PAID IN INK

up overhead, anytime somebody's dead. And they're here to pick the bones, get rich quick and build their thrones.

CLYDE HURLSTON

Masterpiece

There's a bright red light that means record. And so he gets to watch her unsheathe his sword. A tiny piece of gold, is sliding down the track. And her hands engage, so the public won't look back. 'Cause every artist has a masterpiece, that they'll unveil when discussions cease. Just take away the buzz, and flashing lights. And these new lows, will help them reach new heights. Yes, there's that bright red light, and two famous souls at play. While every thrust and pause, takes our ordinary breath away. And we won't press stop, or dare to skip through this. Because there's the slightest chance, there's something that we'll miss. 'Cause every artist has a masterpiece, that they'll unveil when discussions cease. Just take away the buzz, and flashing lights. And these new lows, will help them reach new heights. Don't forget there's a bright red light, and a pile of designer clothes. Here, morals have been replaced, with their success and lofty goals. 'Cause friend, they want the fame, and the growing stacks of green. So it's their most private parts, that'll be displayed until they're seen. Since every artist has a masterpiece, that they'll unveil when discussions cease. Just take away the buzz, and flashing lights. And these new lows, will help them reach new heights. Yes, every artist has a masterpiece. That they'll unveil when discussions cease. Just take away the buzz, and flashing lights. And these new lows, will help them reach new heights. And it's because we long to touch, the ones we see too much. We covet with our mind, those who seem to find. Some genius kind of way, to free what's held at bay. By our sad restraints, so we'll sit back and watch them paint... Their masterpiece.

CLYDE HURLSTON

Here's To Goodbye

This is the story of a girl, who has set out to see the world. She's on her own again. She packs up a few bags, "you'll never see me again," she brags. She's found her strength within. So then she grabs her keys, waves goodbye as she leaves. Some will be left behind, 'cause she's made up her mind. She's gotta get away, and it has to be today! And then she breaks the rearview with her fist. Because she's never felt like this. So now the rearview wears a crack. And friend, she'll be okay. It's because, she won't look back. There's a diner up the road, she has to walk because her car is old. And it's finally broken down. Smoke is pouring out the hood, doubt makes her wonder if this idea was any good. Oh, she's feeling hopeless now. But then she grabs her purse, and as she walks she's feeling worse. But the car is left behind, because she's made up her mind. She's gotta get away, and it has to be today! And she once broke the rearview with her fist. Because she's never felt like this. So now the rearview wears a crack. And friend, she'll be okay. And it's because she won't look back. She tenses as she hears a car approach. She's already running out of hope. And now she wonders who can this be. But she turns and sees her friend, who didn't want her escape to end. So she jumps into the car, and realizes that now they both are free. And so now she breaks the rearview with her fist. Just so her friend could feel like this. So now the rearview wears a crack. And friend, they'll be okay. And it's because, they won't look back.

Modern Day Homicide

Our heart's policemen are undercover, overturning every stone. And interrogating every lover, until we're all left alone. Our trust has been assaulted, battery against our souls. So little tests are armed and ready, protecting us their only goal. But there's really no mystery, as to why our present is history. What could've been was crushed today, by memories it could not outweigh. So now interrogation lamps are burning brightly, blinding the ones we try to know. As we're thinking that we might be, chasing off the ones who'd try to show. That they're not like all the others, who took our hearts and ran. To convince us they will try in vain, 'cause I don't believe they can. For there's really no mystery, as to why our present is history. What could've been was crushed today, by memories it could not outweigh. And there's really no mystery, as to why our present is history. What could've been has surely died, a victim of modern day homicide. Don't you see? The present is a victim of the past, and I'm sure it won't be the last. The future can only be seen in dreams, or in chalk outlines at these crime scenes. So that's why I was able to discover.. That there's really no mystery, as to why our present is history. What could've been was crushed today, by memories it could not outweigh. And so there's really no mystery, as to why our present is history. What could've been has surely died, just another victim of modern day homicide.

CLYDE HURLSTON

All The World's A Stage

If you're hearing this what I'm fearing is, you are trapped inside my mind. And there are things in this forsaken place, that I won't describe as kind. Surely those sights won't outnumber ones, that I'd love for you to see. But they will never grace your eyes, 'cause you have yet to notice me. And still you drift through these corridors, like you were a gentle breeze. Ignoring tales and warning signs, coming and going as you please. But here inside this mind of mine, things are as lucid as they can be. And they're in a constant state of change, to escape the grasp of monotony. Here the roses are a vibrant blue, and the violets bleeding red. And color schemes make little sense, just like the things that once were said. In the form of written words, that I have left upon this page. As a little note you'd take to heart, to prove that all the world's a stage. And the ones in front the audience, will be showered with their cheers. Until your performance finally slips, and you're ostracized for years. Then you'll see the darkened days, that I long to live through here. And the nights won't seem as bright, when the doves fly and spill their tears. And these tears will reflect the stars, that surely used to shine. But whose glow has slowly dimmed, since you are no longer mine. But please don't dress these words, as an attempt to win you back. Rather they are my helpful aids, to reveal the point of view you lack. 'Cause those upon this brittle stage, often never peer behind. The curtain that hides the greedy ones, that will destroy your world in time. And if your hand ever greets the curtain, like a lover's first caress. They will do everything they can, to make sure your soul will never rest. But maybe I'm too paranoid, and I'm overreaching just a bit. But I refuse to believe all I'm told, when I have the guts to question it. But I will leave you to your living, with that spark still in your eyes. Where you can take solace in the fact, the pill you took will match the skies. But my pill matched the violets, that I have once described. And I'll wait for you in this rabbit hole, much to both of our surprise.

CLYDE HURLSTON

Never Behind The Curtain

There are some truths that we will find, and some truths we'll forever seek. And they are some things that we believe, but we wouldn't dare to speak. For we risk being ostracized by those, we say will matter least. Who can override our sense of pride, and bring out our inner beast. For we humans are a foolish lot, who will fight our every urge. Believing that we'll be condemned to hell, so it's our instincts we will purge. And we curse our constant thoughts of lust, as sins better left confessed. And that is why we feel the sting of shame, every time we get undressed. And it's because the weight of guilt, has made us all its' slave. So we look to their provided books, to see how we should behave. But like so many things in this tired world, those books were made by man. Who too engaged in the very sins, they condemned with pen in hand. So when stone is reduced to rubble, and glass reduced to shards. We're just supposed to smile and thank the dealer for our cards. And never question why this hand, has landed on our lives. Ensuring we won't see what's up the sleeve, or see what we're denied. And it's our worldly pleasures, they will call eternal crimes. While singing hymns and wearing grins, 'cause the reasons lack their rhymes. Yet most digest these fallacies, as if they're carved in stone. And thrown down from righteous clouds, to make our world their home. Instead of learning of the councils past, who would sit and then debate. Which new god would win their vote, to rule over every dinner plate. For eating meat on certain days, can escort you to the flames. But most dear souls are blind to see, it's just another of their games. But it's now I will leave you love, for your eyes they long for wool. That was draped across them long ago, so you often beg me not to pull. And it's a request that I will heed, for I know how much you need. To rest your head on what they've said, as you consume your wine and bread. But just recall in the future dear, I tried to help you see the truth. As you were held captive by a fear, that tried to suffocate your youth. So yes, there are many things in life I know, but only one I know for certain. The things you'll accept are only on the stage, and they're never behind the curtain...

CLYDE HURLSTON

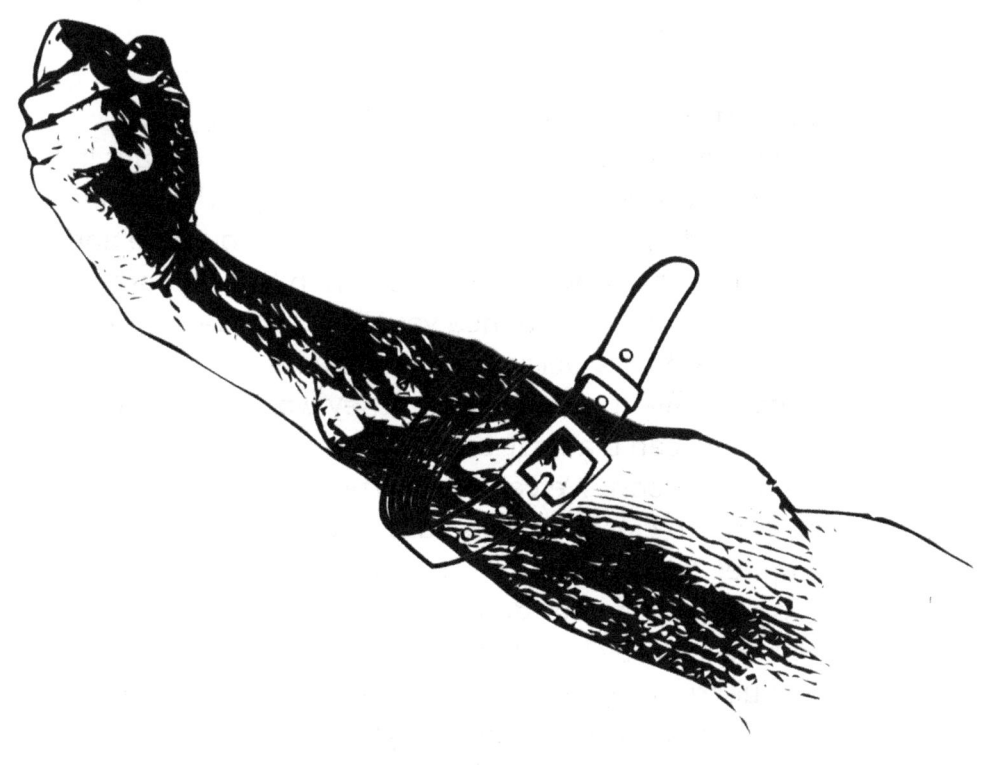

A DEBT PAID IN INK

Under The Influence

Is there some type of music, that you would die to hear? And do you play it loudly, through the speakers loud and clear? Do you treat the lyrics, like commandments from our Lord? While putting on your armor, son you can't forget your sword. Now go get your favorite movie, and let's play it from the start. When things start getting violent, just memorize your favorite part. Then you can reenact it, with your friends and family. As you forget the world is real, and live out your fantasy. And as you rape and plunder, tear this world asunder. Then they'll start to wonder, whose influence you're under. 'Cause we can blame it on a person, we can blame it on a song. We can blame it on a God, and they won't think we're wrong. We can blame it on the books, we can blame it on the screen. We can do anything we want, and get away so clean. Zombies are now the rage, and vampires are a trend. Painting horny boys as wolves, trying to mount your daughters, friend. Now you see them praising evil, and not your god instead. I bet you question sentiments, and wonder where dreams of Heaven went. But missionary's a position, that your precious kids will take. Because their worlds are shaken, watching their parents' marriage break. And with their childhoods now eroded, their sex drives have exploded. And now they're lying on their back, trying to find the love they lack. But if they rape and plunder, and tear this world asunder. Maybe you'll start to wonder, whose influence they're under. 'Cause we can blame it on a person, we can blame it on a song. We can blame it on a God, and they won't think we're wrong. We can blame it on the books, we can blame it on the screen. We can do anything we want, and get away so clean. But we'll just make the art, and leave you to complain. 'Cause killers will be killers, while true artists entertain. So don't blame us for the deeds, and don't bring us to your trials. 'Cause we're not the reason, their names are in your files. Just take a look in mirrors, before your fingers start to point. 'Cause things aren't any clearer, when you've chosen to anoint. Souls with such outdated views, to positions on the court. And my first amendment gets abused, when you need a scapegoat for the sport. But there's not a thing that you can do, except make sure the press is at the scene. Because I want my fifteen minutes starting now, let's turn this nightmare to a dream.

A DEBT PAID IN INK

Victim Of The Scene

As I retract extended hands, I feel you start to slip away. But what no one understands, is you prefer your life this way. Just beyond the reach of those, who seek to make you smile. So you can come and strike a pose, with the vultures for awhile. I'll take the chalk and draw a line, but I have to draw it well. And be sure to take my time, 'cause I have a tale to tell. Someone flashed the red and blues, before I got to spread the news. That if you look she can be seen, 'cause this club has crowned her queen. Yeah, someone flashed the red and blues, before I got to spread the news. That if you look she can be seen, as another victim of the scene. And as you dance in clouds of smoke, your rationale is losing breath. While your inhibitions choke, and self-respect is greeting death. But the beats do hypnotize, the sleeping sheep now awake. I see the bags beneath their eyes, before the day begins to break. So I'll have to take the chalk and draw a line, and I'll have to draw it well. And be sure to take my time, 'cause I have the same, old tale to tell. Someone flashed the red and blues, before I got to spread the news. That if you look she can be seen, 'cause this club has crowned her queen. Yeah, someone flashed the red and blues, before I got to spread the news. That if you look she can be seen, as another victim of the scene. See?Someone flashed the red and blues, the night's favorite pair of hues. But you couldn't care at all, with your hands against the wall. As your body moved in ways, that would impress and then amaze. While someone here's expecting to, spend some time inside of you. While I take the chalk and draw a line, around the girl you used to be. Tonight you'll have yourself a time, but I swear one day you'll see. That someone flashed the red and blues, before I got to spread the news. That if you look she can be seen, 'cause this club has crowned her queen. And she's alive inside the night, because the day don't suit her right. Yeah, they say that she's the crown jewel of the scene, but in truth she's dead inside my dreams...

A DEBT PAID IN INK

What If Life Was A Game

I used to wonder, "What if life was a game, like some handful of cards? Would I play what I'm dealt, and then just give my regards? Or would I slam them down, 'til you reshuffled the set? Like there was no one around, to inflame my sense of regret. Yet every suit has a face, and a sense and a place. But the purse or the pot, is the purpose for the chase. So as the spades meet the clubs, the backs will meet the knives. And envy then becomes, the engine for the lives. But, to know all the rules, you'd have to ask the gods. Because I'm with the fools, that are playing out the odds. And if life is a game, I don't want it to end. 'Cause I took what I had, and I played it my friend. And yeah, it took a toll, and left me covered in dust. But now I'm in control, and I know just who to trust..." Yet still I wonder, "What if life was a game, like some colorful board? Would I be able to move, if we struck an accord? But those things that you stole, as this game wore on. Were the pieces of me, you've built your kingdom upon. Like they were bricks in a wall, that answered every call. That could be placed by the few, in your back row so tall. Compared to the pawns in the front, the bishops in between. Rooks are shaking their heads, they don't know what I mean. 'Cause to know all the rules, you'd have to ask the gods. Because I'm with the fools, that are playing out the odds. And if life is a game, I don't want it to end. 'Cause I took what I had, and I played it, my friend. And yeah, it took a toll, and left me covered in dust. But now I'm in control, and I know just who to trust..." Yeah, you're often playing to win, but there's always a chance. That you'll end with a loss, when you engage in this dance. Moving round we go, may you never lose your way. We'll put a stake in this world, until we're unable to play. But am I safe to conclude, that this path is best? Or did I fail to observe, the wreckage that rests? On the shorelines of lore, where the players lay bare. Or was I too fucking bored, to pay those words any care? Maybe. Because I took my chances anyway...

A DEBT PAID IN INK

In A Time Of Change

I remember quite a time ago, when we liked to take it slow. But the world started moving fast, and the present turned to past. But the things we used to want, just gave way to the things. That we fools put up with now, 'cause nobody ever sings. Sometimes for the better, sometimes for the worse. And I'm sure you would've noticed it, if I hadn't first. But who should bear the blame, when things start getting strange? 'Cause the only thing that stays the same, is that things will always change. And I remember quite a time ago, we were given room to grow. And now we have to keep up with, every fancy little gift. That technology seems to give, to help our generation live. But there's a price we have to pay, when we don't hear a person say. Sometimes for the better, sometimes for the worse. And I'm sure you would've noticed it, if I hadn't first. But who should bear the blame, when things start getting strange? Cause the only thing that stays the same, is that things will always change. And it's with ease we seem to see, the way things always used to be. But a way to replicate the time, is what we never seem to find. So what can we hope to do, after every day is through? But to close our eyes and wish, that people loved to feel like this. 'Cause you can put an "i" in front of everything, and you can put on your silly bling. But friend, it will never take the place, of the look upon your face. During the times you never had a care, and did every crazy thing you dared. But now the kids are way too cool to play, so I doubt we'll ever hear them say. Sometimes for the better, sometimes for the worse. And I'm sure you would've noticed it, if I hadn't first. But who should bear the blame, when things start getting strange? 'Cause the only thing that stays the same, is that no matter what we do, things will always change...

A DEBT PAID IN INK

Can You Describe The View?

I keep thinking to myself, about the way I'm prone to think. And how I've often pushed myself, far beyond the closest brink. But then those thoughts will often turn, in some form to you. And when they're held in retrospect, I was a fool so tried and true. 'Cause I've shared my darkest secrets, until my soul was bare. And when I took a look around, I could see you weren't there. But let me then pick up my pen, and write some words to those. Who were there before you were, and the thorns will outweigh the rose. Won't they, my dear? Girl, you once claimed to want a man, who behaved the way I did. But now I sit and contemplate, about the scars I should've hid. Because that game of show and tell, just made you condescend. And then you turned to walk away, as you brought this to an end. Although I shared my darkest secrets, until my soul was bare. And when I took a look around, I could see you weren't there. But let me then pick up my pen, and write some words to those. Who were there before you were, and the thorns will outweigh the rose. Won't they, my dear? Baby, can you describe the view, from that high horse you're on? 'Cause all it took was rhyming words, and then our bond was gone. Oh, you said I was at fault, and though I disagreed. I would oft apologize, hoping I would then be freed. But instead you chose to linger, on mistakes I may have made. Inferring that it was my words, that left your jealousy displayed. But darling, what am I to do? Ignore this little gift I have? As you put your melodrama on, claiming I tore your heart in half. But how was I to know, that your comfort turned to love? When I was so busy being down, that I couldn't rise above. But you claim you couldn't save, since you weren't a therapist. And here I filed myself as brave, but sadly, I guess the mark was missed...

A DEBT PAID IN INK

Congratulations, Darling.

It's 10:52 p.m. Do you know where my mind is? I'll give you a hint of sorts. It's metaphorically sitting in the finest seat, Of all the nation's courts. It is tense. It is attentive. It is, ready. And you? You're probably not. But I hope you're as relaxed as you can possibly be. As I spit these words at you. Because in truth, they're all I've got. And they are all you deserve, if it's all the same. Why, you ask? It's simple really. (Kind of like you.) It's because I have been waiting the entire day. The entire fucking day. To scour the cracks of my disposition. To dig beneath the layers of banalities, you have used to placate me under false pretense.
In the hopes, I'd find the perfect words to say. That will allow me to properly enunciate my hate. And to purge myself, of your fucking face, that remained in its' most sacred hanging place. In the corner galleries of my mind. But you? You probably couldn't care less. And at first thought, that realization caused a tidal wave of stress. Leaving the mood upon my shore, as misused as a regurgitated mess. But if I could use art to make it right, I would've painted you as obviously oblivious. But that would be another stupid mistake on my part. (Second, only to trusting you.) Because you're not oblivious. You are exact. You are precise. You only play the part of nice. Until it's time for you to play the victim. Then you scream, like the world has got you in a vise. But that's bullshit, baby. Just like most of things you've said to me. Let the words bleed out of me, like an open wound. And then you have something to brag about. But let me mention one, who once shined inside my dreams. Like the

fullest, summer moon. Then magically your x's and o's will change. The x's become crosshairs fixated on my head. While the o's become the noose, slipped around my neck instead. And I am hung in the court of your opinion. Treason, as my crime. And you? Grow a silent as a mime. But pulling your imaginary rope, and building your imaginary box, have both failed to impress. And failed to entertain. They merely delayed the avalanche within me, so your actions were in vain. And you have no one to blame but yourself.

A DEBT PAID IN INK
Strychnine Valentine

If I didn't like how you looked, would I stare as hard as I do? Would I hold back my desire to tear through every part of you? But as I glance at your smirk, and see the look in your eyes. I find this black widow will add, to her collection of flies. And now I'm wondering where this will go next. Does every love affair have to come with side effects? She said, "I think I'd hate you, if I didn't love you so. Don't go too fast now, I just want to love you slow. And though I hate you, I'd still love to make you mine. So won't you promise to be, my strychnine valentine?" I replied, "if you didn't taste so good, would I bother to dine? But what you waste so good, is every second of time. While playing so hard to get, instead of getting me hard. So why would I be surprised, at your blatant disregard?" 'Cause you love to keep me wondering, where this will go next. Does every love affair have to come with side effects? And she said, "I think I'd hate you, if I didn't love you so. Don't go too fast now, I just want to love you slow. And though I hate you, I'd still love to make you mine. So won't you promise to be, my strychnine valentine?" I was caught in a web, that felt so good on my skin. A part of me wants it to stop, the other wants to feel it again. And she said, "every place that you touch, is just another you'll taste. But with every inch that you grow, you start progressing with haste. And you shouldn't talk like big game, unless you wanna be prey. 'Cause once I get on top of you, this is all I will say..." I think I'd hate you, if I didn't love you so. Don't go too fast now, I just want to love you slow. And though I hate you, I'd still love to make you mine. So won't you promise to be, my one and only, strychnine valentine...

Tailor-Made Destinies

Fortify your self-esteem, solidify your selfish ways. Make believe you never dream, and maybe you'll deserve my praise. Because you seem to play a role, that's been tailor-made for you. But dear will you have a soul, when all is said and through? Do you know how it feels to want? Do you know how it feels to need? Do you know any fucking thing, besides the way to make me sing? Don't you know the walls you build, just hide the holes I'd die to fill? But you keep pushing me away, while expecting me to stay. As you play your every field, trying to turn a loss to win. But when you open up your eyes, you'll find that you're alone again. So you can text your saddest tales, to the sympathetic ears. Who'll tell you that it's not your fault, and we're not worth your tears. But people get what they deserve, when the odds are in their view. And still they choose to play a hand, the way that stupid people do. And all I say is… Do you know how it feels to want? Do you know how it feels to need? Do you know any fucking thing, besides the way to make me sing? Don't you know the walls you build, just hide the holes I'd die to fill? But you keep pushing me away, while expecting me to stay. As you play your every field, trying to turn a loss to win. But when you open up your eyes, you'll find that you're alone again…

A DEBT PAID IN INK

Post-Mortem Sensation

When you're on the top, they're claiming that they love you. But get closer to edge, and they're lining up to shove you. Further down the hole, in that spiral going down. And you hit rock bottom, without ever knowing how. Then the limelight fades, and the friends you had in spades. Stopped returning all your calls, and now Belle's not invited to the balls. But that's just how it goes, 'cause everybody knows. You've gotten out of hand, with the powder on your nose. 'Cause too many late nights, have left a case of stage fright. Now paparazzi's pop up, and the flash is blinding you like stage lights. With every flick, they'll take a pic, so you better learn to love it. They often tear you down, and hope you'll rise above it. 'Cause ratings hit a new peak, any time you seem weak. They'll paint a vivid picture, especially if subject matter's bleak. First, you're what they wouldn't wear, they didn't have a care. Until they got the news, you were no longer here. So now they'll raise a glass, and mourn as a nation. As we all hail, the post-mortem sensation. You went and closed your eyes, so now you're on the rise. And it's the kind of thing, that I'm growing to despise. 'Cause when you were alive, allegiance was denied. Then vitals signs took a dive, and they're celebrating you with pride. See an I.V. inside your arm? It wasn't really doing harm. Until it killed Mike, and then poor Amy bit the farm. No shady doctors there, the poor darling was alone. Not picking up the phone, and found later in her home. So no need for candlelights, we knew it all along. She hated rehab, and even said it in a song.

And a mixture of the parts, wreaked havoc on her heart. Now people are cashing in, when the record hits the chart. And then the vultures in the suits, just continue their pursuits. While hoping that even dead tree, keep on bearing fruits. When their hands are wearing blood, in the metaphoric sense. Because they will milk a corpse, until it starts making cents. How fucking sick is that?

A DEBT PAID IN INK

Freedom Through The Press

There's a breeze that mirrors autumn, slowly creeping in the room. As I glance outside the window, the moon has reached it's nightly bloom. But I see a pair of headlights, marching their way into my sight. And it's the owner of this car, who'll be my greatest source tonight. As we make sure she wasn't followed, this clandestine meet resumes. And we exchange the information, that the public just consumes. When it's written in their books, or filtered through their screens. But it's the purpose for this meeting, that helps the end justify the means. And the truth of this sweet matter, was in the details I'd conceal. But my source wants the world to know, their occurrence was for real. It was then her coat became the fall guy, that took it's place upon the ground. As I silenced impending stories, before she ever wrote them down. And like some tyrant for an editor, I removed each article she displayed. As if the suppression of information's best, when the wrong people are dismayed. But each removal then revealed, another hint of godliness. And despite their tightly-fitting forms, they were things I'd hardly miss. For what lies beneath them all, are different paths to Heaven I believe. And there'd be no shortage in the blessings, this sinner would receive. As I was finally granted freedom, my freedom through the press. As in the pressing of her lips to mine, while we made this room a mess. For sheets crashed like tidal waves, and each pillow followed suit. While lamps fell from dresser tops, like a tree had discarded bitter fruit. And there were no witnesses around, nor any statements we could take. We just gave each other every drop, of sweat we could hope to make. As our better parts were so entwined, you'd swear that we combined. But the things she often does to me, can hardly be defined. Much less done justice, by these humble words of mine. For I've weathered storms for this kind of source, and she was surely worth the time...

A DEBT PAID IN INK

Tailor Made For Me

Let your perception of the facts, be the sum of what I am. But darling, never be surprised, when I fail to give a damn. About any single thing, that will ever point to you. For I've grown tired of bleeding out, thanks to your sharpened point of view. And since the blame is thrown around, when the mood will strike you best. These are the times I look down, to see the bullseye's on my chest. So as you lunge to pierce again, I hope you'll choose to peer within. And lay your eyes upon the things, you seem intent on wearing thin. For how am I to heal, when the wound is always fresh? And you mistake my smile for fangs, that will penetrate your flesh. If this is a game, my gorgeous dealer, you must cut the deck for me. Then reshuffle all the cards, as you allow the world to see. That you'll reach deep inside your sleeve, and pull a spade for me. 'Cause it seems the wool I'm hiding in, was tailor made for me. Darling, it seems your life is on a path, that you're quick to show the world. But when it comes to what you've heard, you often to fail to say a word. Before you choose the fabled web, to cast a veil across your doubts. And to start accusing me of things, you'd prefer to do without. And I swear the perception often is, that I'm inclined to the play the game. Of hiding where intention often lives, so dirt is placed atop my name. But I've had a hard enough time, keeping clean when I'm alone. So I'll have to step away from you, when more than stones are being thrown. To let your perception of the facts, be the sum of what I am. So darling, never be surprised, when I fail to give a damn. About any single thing, that will ever make you smile. Since you believe I hope to give you inches, while stealing the most sacred of your miles. And while your past has taught you this, my eyes will paint you as a fool. Who threw away a shade of bliss, 'cause they failed to learn in school. That not every sheep will need a shepherd, nor will a wolf just bare its' teeth. Unless it has the vantage point, and decides it's an easy meal that lies beneath. It's only then will you be devoured.

A DEBT PAID IN INK

At Odds With A Heart

You can take away my reason, and never tell me why. And you can give me only blues, I'll just mistake it for the sky. Then you can say no other grass, gets greener by the week. And I'll never climb the fence, to take myself a peek. But you have to say my name, if I'm asking who you love. And I will look at you, like you were sent from up above. And you have to promise me, that you will never change. 'Cause babe I'd lose my mind, if you started acting strange. 'Cause the moment someone says, that you can't have something. It becomes the only note, your heart will wanna sing. And then you'll have to reconcile, the growing space between. The person in your arms, with the person in your dreams. Babe, you often talk of futures, when the present's still in view. While others use the past, to show what you are prone to do. Like they were tasked to read a list, of history's greatest crimes. That you were guilty of, at least far too many times. But I just can't figure out, whose word I should take. 'Cause it's the kind of choice, that could cause a heart to break. Should I trust the ones who love me, or should I trust the one I love? Who's never done me wrong, and placed no one else above. But the whispers continue growing, to noisy roars inside my ears. And they're intent on resurrecting, the most buried of my fears. But if you tell me that they're lies, I'd believe your every syllable. And ignore the proof before my eyes, of all the shit you'd pull. But really who am I to judge, when you've never done this to me. Knowing if I continued to nudge, I may find myself in misery. But when you're so deep in love, it gets much harder to see. And I've found out how tough, ignoring logic could be. Because I have a working mind, that's at odds with my heart. And the things that I've come to find, may just tear me apart. So if there's someone up there, that's still hearing my cries. Please keep your divine source of truth, because I prefer to keep living these lies. So feel free to call me a fool.

A DEBT PAID IN INK

Predators & Housepets

The smile is often deadly, when flashed to a lonely soul. And it's when you're far from ready, that it's claws have taken hold. But when you're walking unaware, ignorance is closer to the bliss. That causes suns to shine, and makes nights easier to miss. Oh, the eyes are open wide, with so many sights to see. But when you take a look inside, there's a path to misery. So you have to don your armor, to protect your better parts. 'Cause once the ball is rolling, you can't stop it when it starts. And you'll have to guard your heart, or you'll be prone to play the part. 'Cause no matter what you say, we're all a form of prey. For the precious predator, in a housepet sort of wear. So if you're listening, friend, I hope you do beware. The lips are often deadly, when they whisper compliments. And with that shade of lipstick, you'd swear they're heaven sent. And don't let them take the shape, you'd expect to make a kiss. Or else you'll be the next, name right atop her list. But know it doesn't track the naughty, no, it'll only list the nice. Those warm and unsuspecting, yet willing to pay the silent price. Just to be this close to love, with a beauty barely seen. On this duller side of screens, never hearing "cut" behind the scenes. Still there are birds within the trees, and flowers in the garden. But you often fail to see the spiders, that will never beg your pardon. So watch where you place your hands, for the web is unforgiving. And you could be devoured, while the birds continue singing. So the lesson you should learn, is to never mess with nature. Because it will only take a smile, to make you forget the nomenclature. And not leave the butterflies to roam, and fly so very free. 'Cause they once were caterpillars, you never took the time to see. But it's only when they blossom, do they seek to catch your eyes. Leaving a certain kind of Jack, completely lacking in surprise. But in the windows to her soul, often lie the intentions of her mind. And there's a tempered wish for vengeance, that she has come to find. For being broken by the villains, who would spark her inner flame. And leave her crying to the heroes, who sought to save her soul in vain. But to her they were as boring, as watching paint begin to dry. So it's not devoid to reason, why she'd seek to burn alive. And believe me, she won't burn alone.

A DEBT PAID IN INK

The Silent Death Of Doubts

While staring off in space, the world has stopped its' spin. And the movies in your mind, have begun their show again. But before I saw your clothing, take a dive against the floor. I just had this funny feeling, you'd be coming back for more. So I just crossed my fingers, and fronted like I knew. That every time I heard my phone, the text would come from you. Telling me that you were ready, to replay our little scene. After we watched the one or two, that came across our screen. And as the lights began to dim, the dark consumed your frame. I heard your cries for Him, and knew I was to blame. But you can find me guilty, 'cause I'm not innocent. Yet your heaping of this praise, would suggest I'm Heaven sent. But I'd have to disagree, as we spoke between the strokes. I'm just trying to do the things, that had my demons taking notes. 'Cause we made the angels blush, by the time we hit the room. And the sweeter seeds of sin, already were in bloom. So you can ask for blessings, or curse me loud and clear. But either way I'm happy, with what we're doing here. And I'm inclined to think, that if you caught your breath. You'd notice that my doubts, had finally met their death. I see you bite the lips that whisper, just how you want it next. Implying there's a part of you, your favorite part of me neglects. But girl, that's not the case, I just love to hear you beg. As you take my nearest hand, and move it further down your leg. And you made it disappear, beneath the sheets they made to hide. Any pleasant action, that this sinner could provide. And the few kisses that we shared, were long and passionate. As if we feared the taste, would be the last we'd get. Because time, it tore apart, the intentions of the night. By using fabled grains of sand, to slowly bring about the light. And so the day began to break, like a wave across the lake. And in my mind I wondered, how much more pleasure could you take. Because your legs already trembled, and your arms already shook. And your hair fell upon your face, to conceal your blissful look. And you're barely forming words, I hear you giggle as your breathe. But then you see your watch, and you know I have to leave. So you can ask for blessings, or curse me loud and clear. But either way I'm happy, with what we're doing here. And I'm inclined to think, that if you caught your breath. You'd notice that my doubts, had finally met their death…

A DEBT PAID IN INK

A Modern Form Of Bliss

Digging deep beneath the rumors, seems far too great a task. So most would just as well assume, instead of taking time to ask. But luckily for everyone, I'm not like most you call. 'Cause when it's surely said and done, the pendulum swings both ways for all. But whispers are the loudest, when it's you they're talking 'bout. And if they won't repeat themselves, it leads to your walking out. But I would rather watch you walk away, than to take some shit like this. Because I define defiance as a means, a modern form of bliss. And digging deep beneath the questions, is where the answers often lie. But of all the words they like to use, the most seldom used is why. So why should you bother asking things, when it's more fun to criticize? And tear down someone else's pride, while placing your hands upon their prize. 'Cause whispers are the loudest, when it's you they're talking 'bout. And if they won't repeat themselves, it leads to your walking out. But I would rather watch you walk away, than to take some shit like this. Because I define defiance as a means, a modern form of bliss. So sticks and stones may break my bones, yet we know names will always hurt. And nowadays we have even smarter phones, to help with the trafficking of dirt. So take your pics and post them fast, then click the videos to play. 'Cause the first will always be the last, if you believe what the bible has to say. But I don't think that it will ever stop, people and their need for news. Until their names are on another's tongue, and their lives are being used. As fodder for the neighborhood, to share a louder laugh. As they smile and point their fingers, despite their never knowing half. 'Cause whispers are the loudest, when it's you they're talking 'bout. And if they won't repeat themselves, it leads to your walking out. But I would rather watch you walk away, than to take some shit like this. Because I define defiance as a means, a modern form of bliss.

A DEBT PAID IN INK

The Golden Age?

Jesus died at thirty-three, but that just don't mean shit to me. And I think it's time you learn, what really captures my concern. And it's the fact that everyone, may get to feel the sun. But some will turn their final page, when they reach that golden age. See? Robert played his blues guitar, but didn't make it very far. Yet they claim he made a deal, and gave up his soul to steal. While Up On The Roof was Rudy Lew', he was a Drifter tried and true. But sadly he was lined in chalk, before he got to go Under The Boardwalk. And this is the song that I will sing, since the good are dying young. On the stage they left everything, and understood the joy it brung. But here I stand just past the edge, and I keep on looking back. Knowing that it won't be long, until I'm back in black. Brian Jones helped fill our homes, with the sounds of Rolling Stones. And after time he left the band, then he left this God forsaken land. And we all know Jimi left his mark, by playing anthems in the park. Now his innovation's surely missed, since he's in the sky he used to kiss. And oh Janis, she had a voice, that made us all rejoice. But it was the poison in her veins, that took her from this plain. Only sixteen days would separate, their shared and saddened fate. But they will live on inside my head, or my speaker's cries instead. And this is the song that I will sing, since the good are dying young. On the stage they left everything, and understood the joy it brung. But here I stand just past the edge, and I keep on looking back. Knowing that it won't be long, until I'm back in black. During these times, the Days were Strange.

And so often blew the winds of change. But then along came a Rider On The Storm. Who took a Moonlight Drive, and changed the norm. But brother Jim had found his muse. Pamela lit his fire and sparked the fuse. Together they became a funeral pyre. And showed the consequence of getting higher. And so this is the song that I will sing, since the good are dying young. On the stage they left everything, and understood the joy it brung. But here I stand just past the edge, and I keep on looking back. Knowing that it won't be long, until I'm back in black. And they say it wasn't hard to tell, what happened to Jean-Michel. 'Cause although brilliant was his art, the drugs had later played their part. And while we're held captive by words and beats, Mia was killed by a beast stalking city streets. And so The Gits never got their due, and I must write this now for you. And while music eased my pain, fame helped to destroy Kurt Cobain. Was he lost inside the lights? Or did the needle take over on lonely nights? Could he not overcome his past? Did he rise to stardom much too fast? Did he fear his career would not last? Oh, we can still hear that shotgun blast. And then poor Amy swore she wouldn't go, but we all thought it was just for show. Rehab was a catchy song, but we all couldn't be more wrong. It was sad to watch her fade away, when she was blessed with a voice that was made to play. I can still her her bleed through the speakers clear, I bet her family wishes she was still here. But this is the song that we will sing, since the good are always dying young. On the stage they left everything, and understood the joy it brung. But here we stand just past the edge, and we keep on looking back. Knowing that it won't be long, until we're back in black. And so I ask you all, just how sad is that? I have to ask you all, just how sad is that?

CLYDE HURLSTON

Occupy: Yourself

Whether you buy things on release dates, or you're one of many waiting for a sale. The truth is, we're consumers by nature, and our natures will prevail. So while some may seek to nurture, the collections that they own. The shrewd will sell a revolution, to those who feel alone. And the ones who don't realize… The things we really need in life, can't be found upon a shelf. If you really want a revolution, you first have to occupy yourself. So please put down your little signs, unless you're truly for the cause. 'Cause we need to open up our minds, instead of just picking out the flaws. And I think if I could put the letter "i", right there in front of God. Maybe he would be as hard to live without, as your precious pad or pod. But maybe I'm the one that's tripping, because I only bow my head to nod. And I'm out of shape in a culture that, only worships better bods. That are lacking weight upon the waist, and aren't effigies to waste. Or proven products of the food, whose only benefit is taste. But hey, I digress, sorry if I'm not a sheep. I'm just a normal guy with faults, who has to close his eyes to sleep. And I like to talk and question things, that most folks will just accept. And I'll play devil's advocate to those, you claim I should respect. But hey, don't worry, the herd will fall in line. Most are doing it with haste. Thinking that wisdom only comes in tweets, they rush to copy and re-paste. But they don't seem to realize… The things that we really need to hear, must be carried on the breath. Of those who inspire me to live a life, that proves I'm unafraid of death. 'Cause it's alright to laugh, and it's quite alright to smile. But it's when we open up our minds, that life is truly worth the while. See, choosing to join a revolution, after it's already gained its' wheels. Proves that the bandwagon's getting full, no matter how each supporter feels. And the moment the bump that's in the road, decides to rear its' ugly head. The johnny-comes start falling off, and leaves the cause momentum dead. So I truly hope those who choose to occupy, find success and inner peace. And I hope those who wear slogans on a shirt, truly practice what they preach. Or maybe they are only activists, 'cause they want to seem informed. When the fact of the growing matter is, counterculture's now the norm.

CLYDE HURLSTON

What's The Use Of Beauty

My pretentious pretty princess, with a crown that glowed invisible. The ruler of nothing worth anything, who lacked every valued principle. Unaware, every costume that you don, just hides your lack of self-esteem. And the crowd you're following, is the true, pathetic sort of team. Or at least that is what I hear, from those closest to your view. And I believe them to a fault, because the one described is you. And I know just how you are, and it's not good to say the least. Yet when I tried to show the kinder side, you chose to wake the beast. Now you must deal with the consequence, of the actions that you took. Like when you described our interactions, and just how you made me look. How dare you, little darling, to present yourself as this. Talking like I only bothered you, and didn't bring your inner bitch some bliss. When your calls were few and far between, and oft contained a need. So you'd hurl insults at yourself, hoping your ego's what I'd feed. And I fell for it in the beginning, but then I figured out the game. So I began to play it better, and never heard you once complain. Yet, let's not forget the topics, we chose on the lonely nights. When you told me how you liked it, and told me how it was so very tight. Claiming that since you were so small, you didn't always need it large. But when you didn't get what you wanted, you'd reach for your boyfriend that you'd charge. And he'd start dancing where you asked him, causing everything to shake. Giving your toes their familiar curl, until you had all that you could take. And confessions continued coming, like the way you did in my thoughts. But I'll leave some secrets where they lie, 'cause some things should remain between just you and I. But don't take that shade of mercy, as some forgiveness for your crimes. Because you were a waste of my emotions, on so very many times. And now I'm left here to wonder, what's the use of beauty, if there's a fool beneath the smile? And what's the use of duty, if an offered inch becomes a mile? And what's the use of talking, if you have nothing smart to say? And tell me, what's the fucking use of walking, when you wouldn't meet me half the way?

CLYDE HURLSTON

A DEBT PAID IN INK

ACT III:
AMERICAN REQUIEM

CLYDE HURLSTON

A DEBT PAID IN INK

Where The Birds Fear To Fly

There's a land so far away, where the grasses are still green. The sky's a brightened blue, it's such a blissful scene. And there's forest very near, that can inspire words. But if you listened close, not a sound is ever heard. But look to the left, and what do you see? A barbed wire fence, that's as tall as a tree. And the reason for this, is what you'd expect it to be. It's the birth place of death, that only supplied misery. And it's a natural contradiction, to find a place like this. A landscape held in wonder, it could be a place to miss. But when I'm glancing to the sky, friend, I often wonder why. God clearly can't be found, in a place that birds still fear to fly. It was back in nineteen forty-two, when their business saw a boom. But thanks to wretched history, modern flowers fear to bloom. So now the forest has to sit, in complete silence as it grows. Around a God forsaken place, that everybody surely knows. And if you looked to the left, you know what you'd see. A barbed wire fence, that's as tall as a tree. And the reason for this, is what you'd expect it to be. It's the birth place of death, that supplied only misery. And it's a natural contradiction, to find a place like this. A landscape held in wonder, it could be a place to miss. But when I'm glancing to the sky, friend, I often wonder why. God clearly can't be found, in a place that birds still fear to fly. Built on a foundation of fear, while engineering only death. Here the wind barely blows, it comes whispered like breath. The walls are cold to the touch, and chills will greet the spine. For once bigotry screamed proudly, from the most corrupted of minds.

This piece is dedicated to the countless souls lost to us, in the horrors of the Nazi concentration camps.

This poem was inspired by a documentary about the camp at Auschwitz-Birkenau, Poland. But that was by no means the only place that experienced these atrocities, as we all know. We will never forget the lives lost there.

A DEBT PAID IN INK

Oppenheimer's Dream

As I lie awake, my mind replays, the glimpse I had of the end of days. In the brightest flash that eyes could see, leaving smoke and ash where structures used to be. As this place was laid to waste, and left in mouths such an aftertaste. But some people laughed, some people cried. And by a few, silence was supplied. But I was lost in thought, barely took a breath. Then I said aloud, "that I've become death..." And as Hindu scripts came across my lips, I felt a slight pain inside my fingertips. 'Cause the power of fear is what some enjoyed, I sought to create but instead destroyed. And as some rejoiced, my friend I sighed. 'Cause it was then I knew, that the past had died. The world we knew has gone away, thanks to the dream I've dreamed today. And I feel like I should apologize, for the reality before our eyes. The world we knew has gone away, thanks to the dream I've dreamed today. And I feel like nobody cares, as our dreams become nightmares. Some people cried, some people laughed. Gave pats to my back, but didn't know the half. But I was lost in thought as dreams unfurled, then I said aloud, "I'm the destroyer of worlds." 'Cause it was here we sought to test the Trinity, and my expectations were exceed by infinity. Now people call me Father, of what we should abhor. And I want to turn away, but they just demand more. Screaming, "make more bombs, make them fast. In this arms race, we won't choose last. We must be first, so just ignore the costs. We'll just mourn those souls we've lost." In pursuit of our goals, everything we need lies within your dream. No matter how bleak, things here may seem. But as some rejoiced, my friend I sighed. 'Cause it was then I knew, that the past had died. The world we knew has gone away, thanks to the dream I've dreamed today. And I feel like I should apologize, for the reality before our eyes. The world we knew has gone away, thanks to the dream I've dreamed today. And I feel like nobody cares, as our dreams become nightmares.

A DEBT PAID IN INK

A Conformist Prayer

Sitting at my cubicle, just in front a flashing screen. My number was finally pulled, for a meeting with the power team. They gave me documents to shred, and said if not my career was dead. So I thought of my kids in their bed, With these words ringing in my head. I was told that it's divine, to find my place in line. And if my mouth stays closed, I may be the one who's chose. To take a place right by their side, and I only have to lose my pride. And I said yes without a care, 'cause I'm a conformist without a prayer. Now the cross Christ once chose to bear, is on this nifty tie I wear. 'Cause I made the same sacrifice, and I did it for a hefty price. Six figures and a brand new Benz, ignoring what my bosses spend. And with this much who needs a loan, I could make your soul my own. Because I was told that it's divine, to find my place in line. And if my mouth stays closed, I may be the one who's chose. To take a place right by their side, and I only have to lose my pride. And I said yes without a care, 'cause I'm a conformist without a prayer. My soul's stock is hitting lows, but this is the path I chose. You can judge me if you want, but it's not a crime if you don't get caught. So you can turn your nose, but look at the name that's on my clothes. That means that I'm in the upper class, and it's you that I can look past. Because I was told that it's divine, to find my place in line. And if my mouth stays closed, I may be the one who's chose. To take a place right by their side, and I only have to lose my pride. And I said yes without a care, 'cause I'm a conformist without a hope, a wing, or prayer.

Prepared For War

With words sharpened 'til they're blades, I came prepared for war. Knowing it's the close-quarter kind of battle, that you angels do abhor. So with each pointed penetration, I took no solace in the fact. That your resolve was waning, and it wasn't coming back. So I merely spoke and quoted, as the feathers surely flew. Falling in the style of rain, from a heaven I never knew. But who is oft to blame, when courtship turns to crime? Sinking down to the depths, if given a fair amount of time. Or does it even matter, if the blades had found the mark? For the fumes long since sought to rise, all they needed was a spark. Why does tension makes us pretentious? And why does anger makes us righteous? Why does uncertainty makes us weak? And not strong enough to fight this? Some people will blame a devil, and others will thank a god. But I believe the answer's simple, it's because, we're all so very flawed. I have seen the brightest side of down, and traversed the slums of up. And been on the rightest side of wrong, and have been the fool fighting to finally fill, an overflowing cup. I've spat in the face of beauty, and embraced the ugly side of life. And I have carefully chosen my every word, hoping that it will cut you like a knife.

A DEBT PAID IN INK

The Simple Revelation

I have realized that revelations, don't always come from books. Sometimes the revelations come, from simply taking looks. At the wretched souls around you, and the way that they may act. With their perceived possessions, and things they feel they lack. And you'll see they'll go to any lengths, to take the shortest route. And they'll sink to any level, just to see you do without. Oh, friend, the simple revelation is, these people are around. And no, they'll never stop, trying to keep you on the ground. For what's the use of being king, if you have no souls to rule? And what's the use of being smart, if you have no one to play the fool? 'Cause the common folk throughout the world, are plentiful indeed. And they take solace in the fact, it's the working life they lead. 'Cause they'll go to any lengths, to take the shortest route. And they'll sink to any level, just to see you do without. Oh, friend, the simple revelation is, these people are around. And no, they'll never stop, trying to keep you on the ground. So you may want to spread your wings, but they'll clip them with a smile. And they may sell you rocket packs, if you're a good drone for awhile. But just don't expect to share the wealth, that means more to them than life. 'Cause they can pay for better health, after their done feeding on your strife. 'Cause they'll go to any lengths, to take the shortest route. And they'll sink to any level, just to see you do without. Oh, friend, the simple revelation is these people are around. And no, they'll never stop, trying to keep you on the ground. Because these cowards trade in lies, with whomever here will buy. And whispered rumors are supplies, that they have to keep near by. While paying subordinates to stoke the fire, until the bridges start to burn. And some employees are the moths, who never seem to learn. That whatever brings you closer, will burn you in the end. But you'll probably have to be a poser, who'll smile and then pretend. That these flames, they never burned, and this heat, it never frayed. Because you can't afford to skip a payment, on this fancy bed you've made...

Apocalypse At Hand

Time to look beyond the veil, there's more than what you see. And the mind is sitting sail, to where it's supposed to be. In patience we will raise, the anchors from the floor. And shower you with praise, for now and evermore. And this man would gladly sing, if the words would sound as pure. As they do upon your lips, when you say that we'll endure. Dear, is the apocalypse at hand? 'Cause we're losing sight of land. Will we drown inside a sea, that killed who we've tried to be? Or will another rise, to pull you out of this? 'Cause here before my eyes, I've seen the death of bliss. Time to look beyond the wall, as horizons start to blur. Mother Nature wants revenge, for all we've done to her. And there's no fool among us now, who could ever disagree. And say we don't deserve, all that's come to be. And yet this man would gladly sing, if the words would sound as pure. As they do upon your lips, when you say that we'll endure. Dear, is the apocalypse at hand? 'Cause we're losing sight of land. Will we drown inside a sea, that killed who we've tried to be? Or will another rise, to pull you out of this? 'Cause here before my eyes, I've seen the death of bliss.

CLYDE HURLSTON
Look Within

Nowadays it's commonplace
To bow your head and say your grace,
but there are days, when those ways
Aren't worthy of their praise
And it's then that I will ask you
If it's far too great a task to
Keep your head from tilting back
When you feel there's things you lack
Most don't walk, they wish to run
And when the day is said and done
They come to find, they move too fast
The present has become the past
When things get rough on solid ground
And sympathy cannot be found
It's in those times you're stretched too thin
That you should not look up, but rather look within
'Cause nowadays it's become a trend
To give your thanks without an end
But they'll never give him any blame
As they give up credit all the same
So it's now I have to ask you
If it's far too great a task to
Keep your head from tilting back
When you feel there's things you lack
Most don't walk, they wish to run
And when the day is said and done
They come to find, they move too fast
The present has become the past
When things get rough on solid ground
And sympathy cannot be found
It's in those times you're stretched too thin
That you should not look up, but rather look within...

Fail To Fly

Those who see the clouds, will often fear the ground. And those who seek to follow, are often turned around. But when it comes to me, friend, I fear I must admit. That I've often wished to rise, but I've failed at doing it. And now I have myself to blame, for every time I fell. 'Cause I seldom ever tried, and yet I had a tale to tell. But now I'm sick and tired of, each excuse I breathe. So I've buried my desire, and I just forgot to grieve. So throw the dirt and walk away, leave some flowers if you wish. Because I will fail to fly again, with broken wings like this. And as I crash into the ground, you should ignore the sound. Like the tree inside the forest, when nobody is around. And those who seek the journey, may get there in the end. But I've often wished for us, to become more than friends. But there is a tired phrase, about being blind to things. That are often close to you, when that lady finally sings. But now I have myself to blame, for every time I fell. 'Cause I used to hide behind my pride, oh, I wore that armor well. But now I'm sick and tired of, each excuse I breathe. So I've buried my desire, and I just forgot to grieve. So throw the dirt and walk away, leave some flowers if you wish. Because I will fail to fly again, with broken wings like this. And as I crash into the ground, you should ignore the sound. Like the tree inside the forest, when nobody is around.

CLYDE HURLSTON

Raise The Sail

Now I board this boat in awe, as I view the walls I've built. Still held up by hopeless dreams, joined together by the guilt. For letting this accident, that some have labeled life. To weigh my disposition down, and choke my hope with strife. But I'm still broadcasting live, from the length of arms you own. And still you won't come take a dive, into what you call a sacred zone. So I'll raise the sail and wait, for you to change your mind. But with the water pouring in, I beg you not to take your time. And yes I chose to paint the walls, with shades of bitterness. I think the image of your face, is a sight I'll never miss. Because I carry you with me, each time the seas rebel. And the heart that's on my sleeve, seems like it's beating well. So I'm still broadcasting live, from the length of arms you own. And still you won't come take a dive, in this supposed sacred zone. So I'll raise the sail and wait, for you to change your mind. But with the water pouring in, I beg you not to take your time. I wonder if you'd penetrate the walls, I've taken years to build. To resuscitate the self-esteem, this world has slowly killed. Or would you merely wish to see, the horrors on your own. As my wounds were sure displayed, during this time I've been alone. But I feel a change within the wind, as the degrees begin to rise. To make it seem a lot less cold, as the clouds retake the skies. From the grips of metaphoric hands, that were owned by darkened nights. Who chased away the darling stars, and then revoked their rights. Like the right to shine within your eyes, as you smile a smile at me. As if to say there'll be a day, when I'd wake beside you finally. But until then... I'm still broadcasting live, from the length of arms you own. And still you won't come take a dive, into what you call a sacred zone. So I'll raise the sail and wait, for you to change your mind. But with the water pouring in, I beg you not to take your time.

CLYDE HURLSTON

Reinvent The Wheel

Is your life all plotted out? Do bullet points fill your days? Is there a list of used excuses, that could justify your ways? 'Cause I often watch and wonder, if you ever had remorse. Or do you play it all by ear, then let nature take its' course. As you try to reinvent the wheel, and ignore the things you feel. But as that wheel begins to roll, I see you start to lose control. So you can try to hold the water, or even catch a flame. Oh, you can try your everything, the result will be the same. So scribble outside the margin, maybe color outside the lines. And instead of saying sorry, just keep changing with the times. But that doesn't seem to suit you, or even fit you very well. So your life maybe the story, that your fellow fools will tell. As you try to reinvent the wheel, and ignore the things you feel. But as that wheel begins to roll, I see you start to lose control. So you can try to hold the water, or even catch a flame. Oh, you can try your everything, but the result will be the same. Now while some forget the past, they seem doomed to just repeat. The future will be undermined, by the foolishness beneath. If you took a look at the present, and see how far it's gotten you. As I fight to hide my laughter, while I just sit back, watching you. As you try to reinvent the wheel, and ignore the things you feel. But as that wheel begins to roll, I see you start to lose control. So you can try to hold the water, or even catch a flame. Oh, you can try your everything, but the result will forever be the same.

A DEBT PAID IN INK

Bear The Weight

The song of running water, is so soothing of a sound. Yet it's come to symbolize, each tear that hit the ground. When that look upon your face, was frozen into place. By mistakes I may have made, that left this aftertaste. Darling, it's not fair for you, to bear the weight for me. So I think it may be best, if you got away from me. To save you the despair, and save you all the pain. That you would probably feel, if you returned to me again. 'Cause the sound of burning pictures, is like music to a moth. And baby, we are not the same, for we're cut from different cloth. But to me that doesn't mean, that I can't love your brand. But the things inside my head, are things you'll never understand. So it's not fair for you, to bear the weight for me. And I think it may be best, if you got away from me. To save you the despair, and save you from the pain. That you're guaranteed to feel, if you returned to me again. I've seen you pulling out your hair, and shedding tears alone. But the part of me that's here, is yours to love and own. But the part of me that's lost, for years has gone unfound. And I've paid a tremendous cost, because you're not around. But baby, I don't blame you, in truth, I'd do the same. 'Cause the one you love don't love himself, so how can you win this game? When it's not fair for you, to bear the weight for me. And I think it may be best, if you stayed away from me. To save you the despair, and save you all the pain. That you would probably feel, if you returned to me again. Oh, that maybe a poor choice of words, but I'm just honest after all. And I know you'll still be there, to try and catch me if I fall. But I'm raining broken pieces, and I don't want to slice your skin. So darling you will have to move, and let me kiss the ground again. 'Cause I'd rather die than hurt you, though it seems I truly have. But I ask of you to hate me not, 'cause your love is all I ever had. And despite all I'll never be, I thank you for all you've shared. Because in the end you've proved, that at least one person truly cared.

A DEBT PAID IN INK

Branded With Welcome

I'm on a journey in life, without the aid of a guide. I've buried too many things, too far deep inside. It's long past the time, I climbed out of this hole. And set these burning brown eyes, on some kind of goal. But now my anger has grown, far beyond my control. And I'm lacking the words, to soothe or console. So get out of my way, unless you want to ride. Once a path has been cleared, just know I won't be denied. But if you're re-tracing my history, until the footnotes are read. It will be typed up in bold, that mister nice guy is dead. 'Cause I was down in the dirt, when you'd cross my back. Like I was branded with welcome, and was some kind of mat. But if life is nothing but a race, then I'm unfit for second place. So when the light turns to green, you'll enjoy what you've seen. But don't dare say to me, that's it's all been a dream. Or else my engine won't be alone, whenever it screams. Girl, I gave in to the whispers, of well-reasoned voices. That would always remind me, when it came to your choices. I was never your first, but I should be your best. Now you've brought out my worst, and proved you're just like the rest. So I'll close my eyes, and put my hands on my ears. So I won't hear or witness, all of your foolish tears. But if you're re-tracing my history, until the footnotes are read. It will be typed up in bold, that mister nice guy is dead. 'Cause I was down in the dirt, when you'd cross my back. Like I was branded with welcome, and was some kind of mat. But if life is nothing but a race, then I'm unfit for second place. So when the light turns to green, you'll enjoy what you've seen.

But don't dare say to me, that's it's all been a dream. Or else my engine won't be alone, whenever it screams. Now I'm regaining a measure, of my confidence. So karma has come 'round, to bring you consequence.

The Darker Parts Of Me

It's often been inferred, or whispered for a bit. But the truth is obvious, if you really look for it. See, something's wrong with me, it's what you'll come to learn. But you can let it be, there's no cause for your concern. 'Cause my insecurities, have often been displayed. The public's used to them, so their opinion's never swayed. And the faults I tried to hide, are here for all to see. In a place where shades of happiness, are drowned in the darker parts of me. It's always asked of me, in a soft and sweet request. That I should behave in ways, most people would suggest. But they're just being nice, and overlooking ugliness. So they'll often pay the price, for my years of bitterness. 'Cause my insecurities, have often been displayed. The public's used to them, so their opinion's never swayed. And the faults I tried to hide, are here for all to see. In a place where shades of happiness, are drowned in the darker parts of me. Oh, every mental scene, that I'd care to recall. Upsets me because, I hate that sight of them all. And no matter what they say, this is the way it will stay. Unless some force comes along, and turns the tide the other way. 'Cause my insecurities, have often been displayed. The public's used to them, so their opinion's never swayed. And the faults I tried to hide, are here for all to see. In a place where shades of happiness, are drowned in the darker parts of me.

CLYDE HURLSTON

Wishing Well

Within a distance ever-growing, there lies a great divide. Such a precipice between us, that only the blind have denied. But my eyes have slowly opened, felt the weight of both of the lids. I tried to continue with the hoping, but forgot who I was trying to kid. And now I'd be lying if I said, the walls aren't growing closer by the day. Because they still display the mark, of where your framed picture would lay. But now, I'm alone and singing, "Has the water turned to wine, since we finally gave it time? I guess the vein you cut was mine, left this rose severed at the vine. But there's one story left to tell, of how I want to wish you well. But it seems I keep forgetting, that my heart's not letting..." So now I'll take my pretty penny, and throw it gently down the hole. Watch it shimmer in the darkness, like you did inside my soul. But the well is lacking water, it's only filling with clichés. And to ignore them is getting harder, since nights have drowned the days. And now, I'd be lying if I said, that I don't miss the smell of your perfume. 'Cause if I was led here by the scent, I would find your grace in every room. But now, I'm alone and singing, "Has the water turned to wine, since we finally gave it time? I guess the vein you cut was mine, left this rose severed at the vine. But there's one story left to tell, of how I want to wish you well. But it seems I keep forgetting, that my heart's not letting..." So my displays of loving this, have been replaced by loneliness. And my thoughts of waking bliss, have been put to sleep by bitterness. And the smile that's on your face, as you find another in the breeze. Makes me hate the very wind, that's sure to penetrate the trees. On this lovely autumn day, that feels of winter's touch. As I watch you use your faith, as each arm's respective crutch. 'Cause you've been leaning on things, you've believed for very long. As proof there's a love beyond the clouds, that has helped to make you strong. But dear, whatever floats your boat, And helps you sleep at night. May never be described as wrong, but it surely doesn't make it right. So go rushing to your altar, and be sure to spew recycled vows. As those of you left, laugh through the raising of our brows.

CLYDE HURLSTON

The Promise Of Disaster

Woke up to a shining sun, and no brimstone was to be seen. I expected fire in the skies, not a display I would call serene. But the calendar was screaming May, with a big, black twenty-one. So I fear it'll be the same old thing, when this day is said and done. 'Cause the promise of disaster, seems to bright to us. That we'll point to Nostradamus, to show how right he was. But those are just poetic words, written down by a man. Who thought his use of symbols, would help you understand. But if you ever stopped to see, what's behind the prophecy. You'd know every tale about the end, starts in the imagination, friend. So if you look behind the curtain, and saw the truth with your own eyes. You'd probably know for certain, there's meaning behind the guise. But was the writing closet drama, or was a theatre to be blessed? With performances as grand, as Emperor Constantine's request. For them to gather in a circle, and find a tighter line to tow. So a book could be created, and sold to the ones who didn't know. That the promise of disaster, seems to bright to us. That some point to dear, old John, to show how right he was. But those are just poetic words, written down by a man. Who thought his use of symbols, would help you understand. But if you ever stopped to see, what's behind the prophecy. You'd know every tale about the end, starts in the imagination, friend. So if you look behind the curtain, and saw the truth with your own eyes. You'd probably know for certain, there's meaning behind the guise. When interpretation's often fluid, we see many avenues are filled. And vague's the order of the day, so intentions are never spilled. For in the days we see as past, art could secure an early death. If the word we know as heresy, was carried loudly on a breath. By one who's only mission, was to secure obedience and rule. And thought enlightened artists, would surely paint him as a fool. But he never once stopped to think, of the gift that knowledge could be. He only remembered it was forbidden, to be eaten from the tree. 'Cause the promise of disaster, seems to bright to us. That they'll often point to Eve, and curse the blight she was. But those are just pathetic words, often uttered by a man. Who never thought the use of symbols, would help him understand. But if you ever stopped to see, what's behind the prophecy. You'd know every tale about the end, starts in the imagination, friend. So if you look behind the curtain, and saw the truth with your own eyes. You'd probably know for certain, there's meaning behind the guise. Just ask our darling Mary, if the historians are kind. Or ask those who sought to catch a comet, to tell us what we'd find. If we ever stopped to look behind the curtain, and saw the truth with our own eyes. They'd say we'd know for certain, there's meaning behind the guise. And the truth is those in power, will do anything to stay. So they'll invent the words, they claim the Lord would say. And as we lie beneath their thumb, we'll focus only on our plight. And we'll forget that our own futures, could be brighter than the stars at night. 'Cause the promise of disaster, seems to alright to us. As long as we can check our status, while the others fight and fuss. 'Cause we are just apathetic herds, often gathering in mass. Who never

thought the use of symbols, would ensure our place,
in this country's lower class...

A DEBT PAID IN INK

Overrun By Weeds

Thick on a summer afternoon, is how the air begins to feel. So I'm staring at the sun, hoping this heat is not for real. But the sweat upon my brow, dissolves the thoughts of dreams. And the street's so desolate, you could paint an Armageddon scene. But I still spend my everyday, locked deep inside my head. Wondering if I'll ever find a way, to take back the things I said. But the echoes of the door, are ringing through the halls. 'Cause she don't live anymore, and she won't return my calls. Oh, the cure for loneliness, is what everybody needs. But my heart's the empty home, that's overrun by weeds. So the ghost inside this house, will haunt his every room. Until he's finally covered up, by whatever is in bloom. Layered thick upon my tongue, was once a story full of bull. That I just had to tell, as if it was my final card to pull. But she looked in my eyes, and saw through all the lies. And while fighting back the tears, she unraveled all the ties. So now I spend my everyday, locked deep inside my head. Wondering if I'll ever find a way, to take back the things I said. But the echoes of the door, are ringing through the halls. 'Cause she don't live anymore, and she won't return my calls. Oh, the cure for loneliness, is what everybody needs. But my heart's the empty home, that's overrun by weeds. So the ghost inside this house, will haunt his every room. Until he's finally covered up, by whatever is in bloom. See, the vines will climb the walls, to give the house some shade. While behind the drapes I hide, this wretched bed I've made. As I sit inside my chair, drowning sorrow in despair. This house of cards could fall, and Lord, I wouldn't even care. 'Cause I can't make her see, I'm not who I used to be. And I can't reclaim the love, that's been denied to me. I took her for granted once, and overlooked her twice. The third time's not a charm, 'cause this hell ain't very nice. For I'm a victim of circumstance, that's what I used to claim. But that's a foolish man's chosen dance, so now I'll take all the blame. I came home late too much, if I even came at all. Yet I wondered why her touch, mirrored the season after fall. But now I know the truth, so place the dunce's cap on me. Because of foolishness, alone is what I'll have to be

A DEBT PAID IN INK

Let The Inferno Subside?

My imagination has set sail, on a sea that moves like dust for you. But I ponder what will prevail, is it my trust or my lust for you? For I hear you whisper words, that sound sweet when laced in breath. And so my fear of offending God, has slowly faced it's death. For my hands, they wish to tear the lace, away from your temple, love. Since we don't have the time to waste, oh, the concept's simple, love. But if you knew the things, my mind chooses to recall. I believe the one you're with, well, he wouldn't like me at all. But it's no fault of my own, 'cause you know what you did. And now these memories replay, while you continue to live. In an oblivious bliss, to the improvements I've made. But if I ever get the chance, best believe they will be displayed. For what once was a Sliver, has both blossomed and grown. And this Enigma you've solved, still has so much to be shown. 'Cause the humble are willing to learn, if you're still willing to teach. And I feel I've made strides, but you're still so far from my reach. So what am I to do, when the passion does ignite? And I want to feel you again, but only the stars are shining at night. Should I let the inferno subside, or should I pick up the phone? And whisper to you, that, "I hope you're alone." But I know that you're not, first hand it would seem. 'Cause there's evidence abound, that you're living out your dream. And the pride I feel for you, is something you've earned. And yet, I haven't gotten over you, that's something I've learned. So tell me how it feels to know, that I wrestle with lust and despair. And the few that I've pleased, still have failed to compare. To the few nights that i had, in the web surrounded by flame. That felt like silk to the touch, yes, to leave was a shame. But I was too immature, and too afraid of the risk. Of feeling something for you, and so my departure was brisk. But I've apologized, while you always forgave. And now I long for that night, when I was both a king and a slave.

A DEBT PAID IN INK

And The Villain Said Unto Him...

Life is but a stage. And on it, we are but bit players. In a beautifully, glorious tragedy. And in this, some people are stars. Some people are merely stagehands. And a greater number are anonymous extras. But from the moment the curtain meets the air, there is going to be a time. No matter how well the lines are read. No matter how compelling the story may seem. And no matter how long the performance lasts. Despite the fact, that time sometimes seems to stop. There will be a time, when the curtain must come down. And then, all that we have known, is at its' end. But, it's while on this stage of life, most believe they are performing to an audience of one. A one that has many names. Whether he is the Unseen Director. Or the so-called, Great Architect. Some call him The Creator, while some merely call him God. And there are some who choose to get more personal, by giving a proper name, to what is otherwise, impersonal. They are like you hero. They are greatest form of fodder in this universe. They are the fools. Fools that find their strength in the hollow. The hollow creation of man, most know as faith. To those who have been spared the reality of suffering, faith is but a blissful fantasy. A fantasy that they believe to be the true way of the world. But it is we, the enlightened, who have suffered, that know the truth. And the truth is, faith is nothing more than lies. Surely-sweetened lies, spoon-fed to the masses, like a form of metaphoric food. And those with the wool across their eyes, believe themselves to be full. Thinking that this food, is their true sustenance. And the only thing they will ever need to survive. But that is merely another lie. And it is here, that I wait, patiently, for their fantasy to crumble into ash. As the weight of reality, crashes through their perfect world. Like a wrecking ball sent to level, that which is no longer safe to stand. And is THEN, that their souls will see their food is but a tease. A tease that has left a hole in them, that no soul can fill. A hunger that no amount of nourishment, will ever seem to satiate. And I will laugh. I will laugh until the tears fall from my eyes like rain. And as those drops hit the ground, they will water the seeds. The seeds of bitterness, already planted in your mind. The same seeds that have long since blossomed in mine. And have born fruit in many forms. And your God, if he exists, knows how sweet this fruit can be. For your good book hero, it claims He is far more vengeful than we. It claims that he is merciful, yet he'll send the imperfect to hell. And we all know He is jealous. So hide your golden bull hero, you better hide them well. For you wish not to face the wrath, of these collected contradictions. But enough about him. Let's talk about you hero. You believe yourself to be always in the right. Therefore you believe your actions to be righteous. But what they really are, is simple. They are the reflection of the society you claim to serve. They are SELF-righteous. You see, a true hero does what he or she knows is right. They often do it, seeking no benefit. They do not seek publicity. They only seek anonymity. They do not wear a cape. They do not wear a badge. Whether it's with a medical kit, or a stack of books, they improve the quality of life in a given place. And what do you do hero? You claim to catch criminals, but all you caught was gossip. You wish to make improvements, but you only made the headlines. And you seek to make them safe, yet you've only secured your status. You are a hypocrite, hero. As hypocritical as that one you believe is sitting on a cloud. The one, who to prove his love, willingly sacrificed his son. And you call ME a monster? HA! But here's the kicker. He claims he did it, just to save a wretch like me. Oh hero, that is truly, an amazing grace. Or how ever that stupid song goes. The bottom line is this. We are but two sides to the same coin. I make no attempts to hide my flaws. You've drowned yours in mask and cape. But it's okay hero. I've escaped your grasp before, and I shall do it again. Haven't you heard? The curtain is still up. But when we get to that last chapter hero, you will have to choose. Whether you need your halo, or if you need your horns. Because your slaps on the wrist only amuse me. One of these days, you will need those nine inch nails, to put me up for good…

CLYDE HURLSTON

Dreams To Life

On the days I'm not fond of life, I will tend to close my eyes. Trying to forget the ache of strife, and to pacify a mind with lies. But reality is seeping in, like the brightest shade of light. And this bed I'm sleeping in, seems its' emptiest tonight. But there's no difference made, when we call a spade a spade. 'Cause dear I have been weighed, and still found wanting you. So if I told you a secret, would you be able to keep it? 'Cause there's this thing that I do, when I'm thinking of you. And if I'm at home, and I feel so alone. Then I reach for your picture, and I make you my own.
But it's on days like this, that I'm not fond of truth. 'Cause it stains displays of bliss, with signs of fleeting youth. And the lines upon my face, are both subtle and profound. Yet there's still time to waste, as I picture your clothing on the ground. Girl, it's on days like this, that I really do believe. That I'm preferring dreams to life, and I'm so easy to deceive. 'Cause you'd never feel for me, the way I feel for you. But when I close my eyes, you'll love me 'til I'm through. And whether you do regard, me as any kind of friend. It'll never be enough, so don't expect me to pretend. That I am ever satisfied, in any role beside your king. 'Cause another part of me has died, and yet you barely see a thing. 'Cause your stare is occupied, by some other wretched soul. And yet it's only thoughts of you, that can seem to make me whole. So if my hand's moving to a rhythm, please don't think me any less. Since it's only in my mind, that I'll get underneath your dress. And if this revelation, makes

you feel any sort of way. Know I've dreamed and bended you, in every single sort of way. And when my head hit the pillow, and my eyes closed to night. I was then the lucky fellow, who could feel your love was tight. But darling, tell me what's a picture, when the subject is compared. To this state of loneliness, whose hold is cold and bare. And know when I close my eyes, your face is everywhere. And while you're far beyond my reach, these words are far beyond your care.

CLYDE HURLSTON

Learned To Lack

There's a laundry list of things, that I once wished to say. But doubt came crawling in, to steal my words away. But if I ever found the strength, to say just how I feel. Girl, I'd have to know if you, could tell I was for real. Darling, open up your eyes, and shine that blue my way. Because deep inside my skies, all I ever see is gray. And when clouds come rolling in, and that sky just turns to black. I hope you'll look the past the things, that I haven't learned to lack. There's a laundry list of things, I once wished to do to you. But my disappointment sings, the same old song that's true. About a boy who loves a girl, but that girl loves somebody else. And he tried to change her mind, but got caught up in a mess. Every time she opened up her eyes, and shined that blue his way. Because deep inside his skies, all he ever saw was gray. And when clouds come rolling in, and that sky just turned to black. She didn't look the past the things, that he never learned to lack. Listen and I will sing it clear, this boy was a victim of his fear. Seems he couldn't live without, playing victim to his doubts. And it was his lack of self-esteem, that stopped his chasing of a dream. And that girl saw every bit of this, and so she never kissed his lips. Nor did she ever open up her eyes, and shine a shade of blue his way. Because deep inside his broken skies, all he ever chose to see was gray. And when the clouds come rolling in, and that sky just turned to black. He could never look the past the things, that he felt others thought he lacked.

A DEBT PAID IN INK

With A Preacher's Zeal, I Screamed

I feel you twist my words, the way you'd twist a vine. I see you hide your point of views, to try and make them mine. Friend, I see your sense of self, is growing by the day. And that book upon the shelf, has gotten in your way. So recite your every scripture, and sing your every verse. Thinking if we died today, you'd be rewarded first. But if you stopped to look, I think you'd finally see. That you and I are not alike, and that's alright with me. I see you at your pulpit, in front of opened eyes. And ears that are the culprits, who digest the spoken lies. You have masked as answers, to the questions we may have. But it's your claims that make me smile, and slowly start to laugh. As you recite your every scripture, and sing your every verse. Thinking if we died today, you'd be rewarded first. But if you stopped to look, I think you'd finally see. That you and I are not alike, and that's alright with me. And then he finally turned to me, with a look of disbelief. As if it were my words, that showered him in grief. But now I've got his whole attention, just as I had dreamed. And it was with a preacher's zeal, That I finally went and screamed. "You have no right to judge me, for you are not my Lord. And the things I choose to do, are of my own accord. So you can save your saving, for those who need it most. 'Cause I've done alright without you, and I don't mean to boast." And as my words began to echo, I could feel the tension rise. As if I said the words, that unlocked some kind of prize. 'Cause if there is a God, I'm sure I've earned his spite. But just because I've wronged, friend, it doesn't make you right. For there's no price I wouldn't pay, just to own my soul. But to me that doesn't mean, I must be under your control. So you can enjoy the view, when looking down your nose. But your frame of mind's too small, to hold my current pose. 'Cause it's here I stand alone, on a trail that I have blazed. Right through the potter's field, you sheep have proudly grazed…

A DEBT PAID IN INK

Bow Before My Nothing

I see you look so close to perfect, and then I feel my stomach turn. But how to hold my hate within, is what I still fight to learn. But then I see the sparkle in your eyes, and it's no secret that I yearn. To slowly pull and tear it out, and then watch as your forests burn. Then I'd say fuck your fallen tears, fuck your hopes and dreams and fears. 'Cause you deserve to be alone, or in a heap before my throne. But there's no crown upon this head, so I rule with angry words instead. And I hate all that you are, getting on your knees will get you far. And there's no crown upon this head, my soul and faith are half past dead. So you can stand for something, but you will bow before my nothing. Now you see me look close to hideous, and then you start to crack a smile. Because you know I'll never change, and if I did, it'd take awhile. But then you see the walls I've built, my wretched monuments to guilt. And they're far too big for you to scale, 'cause we know you can't break a nail. Then I'd say fuck everything you've thought, while pouring gas on all you've bought. And then I'd surely strike a match, toss it your way and whisper, "catch…" But there's no crown upon this head, so I rule with angry words instead. And I hate all that you are, getting on your knees will get you far. And there's no crown upon this head, my soul and faith are half past dead. So you can stand for something, but you will bow before my nothing. So don't compare me to your equals, 'cause I won't last until the sequels. This is a once-in-a-lifetime kinda hate, the in-a-blaze-ofglory kinda fate. 'Cause I gotta gift you can't redeem, and the nightmare's overrun the dream. So you can get on your knees and pray, but you'd only be an object in the way. Then I'd say fuck all your whispered prayers, save your faux concerns and tarnished cares. I don't need anything but another breath, 'cause I refuse to be another early death.

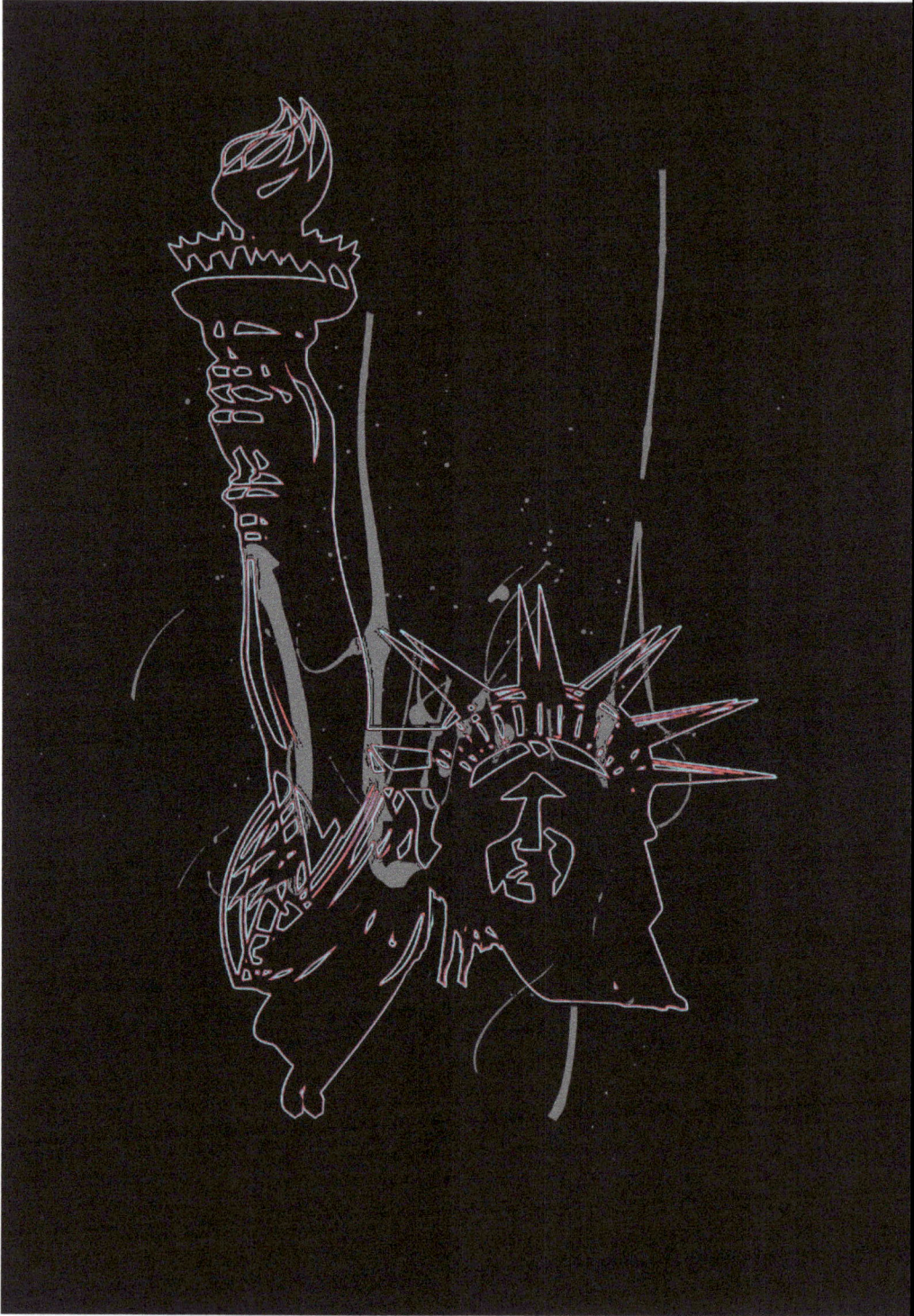

CLYDE HURLSTON

American Requiem

Turning on the nightly news, has become a greater task. That it ever used to be, because I really hate to ask. What's going on inside a world, that I don't recognize? Since we watched our decency, be bid on like a prize. But if you're inclined to pay, they can make it go your way. But if you're asking me, this is all I have to say. 'Cause there used to be a day, when the children did believe. That with a pair of open arms, is how they'd be received. But now every warm embrace, has grown much colder. As they finally woke to see, that our dream was over. So say goodbye to red, goodbye to white. The wrong has overcome what's right. I'll say goodbye to blue, goodbye to you. It's the only thing we have left to do. Say goodbye to stripes, goodbye to stars. They've taken everything once ours. Say goodbye to God, goodbye to souls. The vultures have achieved their goals. And I feel guilty often times, for being creative with my lines. 'Cause underneath the bridge, a man is creative with his signs. And I know it's not my fault, but it doesn't stop the hurt. That I see behind his eyes, as he wipes away the dirt. Yet if you're inclined to pay, you could make him go away. But if you're asking me, this is all I have to say. I remember when there used to be a day, when that man did believe. That with a pair of open arms, is how he'd be received. But now every warm embrace, has grown much colder. As he finally woke to see, that our dream was over. So say goodbye to red, goodbye to white. The wrong has overcome what's right. And I'll say goodbye to blue, goodbye to you. It's the only thing we have left to do. Say goodbye to stripes, goodbye to stars. They've taken everything once ours. Say goodbye to God, goodbye to souls. The vultures have achieved their goals. Now I hear the market's on the rocks, and the shops are closing down. And you'd see houses up for sale, if you took a look around. But gold is reaching highs, as morale is hitting lows. And where we'll go from here, is what nobody really knows. But what the experts often say, is things will go our way. But we have to give it time, and find our place in line...

CLYDE HURLSTON

Is The Cycle Broken?

It seems we're drawing circles, leaving the same old motions made. And we're still treading water, raising our heads as we wade. And it's like we each missed a dose, of our Dramamine. And it's this merry-go-round, that's the stage for our drama scene. But since someone's drawn the curtain, I'll have to man the lights. 'Cause it seems we're on the path, toward our epic fights. But as the volume starts to rise, can you look me in my eyes? And say the cycle's broken, until it doesn't sound like lies? Now it seems you're building walls, so how can the fences mend. When I can't keep up construction, as you smile and just pretend. That we didn't miss a dose, of some sweet reality. Knowing I can't quite figure out, why you're so fucking mad at me. But someone's drawn the curtain, so I have to man the lights. 'Cause it seems we're on the path, toward our epic fights. And as the volume starts to rise, can you look me in my eyes? Then say the cycle's broken, until it doesn't sound like lies? Oh, it seems I've crossed the line, by suggesting moving on. And you can tell I'm serious, now that what you've drawn is gone. 'Cause we don't need another dose, of those jagged little pills. That some labeled memories, our minds have had their fills. But you just like bringing up, my every wrong in sight. Pretending every right has danced, in the shadow of the night. And I'm not laying blame, or impersonating saints. I'm just digging for the truth, beneath a layer of complaints. But you won't say a word, and it's as if you know. That I have some psychic powers, that I've refused to show. But we we're too old for this, and not getting any younger. So can we get back to the bliss, for which I've begun to hunger? Or is your soul content, to starve us of happiness? While neglecting all the parts, we have to clean inside this fucking mess. But someone's drawn the curtain, so I have to man the lights. 'Cause it seems we're on the path, toward our epic fights. And as the volume starts to rise, can you look me in my eyes? Then say the cycle's broken, until it doesn't sound like lies? Baby, tell me, is the cycle broken? Or are those pieces from our hearts?"

CLYDE HURLSTON

One Wish

If wings were our arms, how high would we fly? As clouds work their charms, inside this blue sky. I glance at your smile, it fills me with pride. To know I've come this far, and I haven't died. But if I had one wish, it would be this. That your wings would always work, during the bitter times that you're not in mines. If clouds were our bed, how well would we sleep? Seeing sunshine instead, of the darkness I keep. Locked in my heart, before you arrived. And chased it away, and made me feel alive. But if I had one wish, it would be this. That your wings would always work. During the bitter times, that you're not in mines. Yes, if I had one wish, it would be this. That your wings would always work. During the bitter times, so you'd be free from your hurt. 'Cause hurt I know well, it's shown it's face. To me in my hell, as I burned in my space. But you killed the flames, with the light in your eyes. Proving it's not the result, but the fight in my tries. So as I write these words, you dance in my mind. The image preserved, one flash at a time. So I'll greet today, with strengthened resolve. Since it was my pain, that your love dissolved. And that's why if I had one wish, it would be this. That your wings would always work. During the bitter times, that you're not in mines. Yes, if I had one wish, it would be this. That your wings would always work. During the bitter times, so you'd be free from your hurt. Now I'm free from myself, free just to fly. And I'll tell the world, so they'll know why. It's because of you, and the things that you do. So when I'm laid to rest, and my life is through. Just know that

I gave you my all, and I'll pray that you'll never fall. So baby, keep flying high. It's only for now, since there's never goodbye. 'Cause if I had one wish, it would be this. That your wings would always work. During the bitter times, that you're not in mines. Yes, if I had one wish, it would be this. That your wings would always work. During the bitter times, so you'd be free from your hurt...

CLYDE HURLSTON
An Imagined Nation

Darling, imagine if you will, a vast display of land. And the sun is touching every place, a man could surely stand. Then imagine that this place, was locked deep inside a mind. That was like the rabbit hole of lore, with wonders for you to find. Would you drink the offered tea, to help swallow chosen pills? Or would you take the hookah for a whirl, to see if you could feel the thrills? Would you see how far the path, laid before you has to go? Or shall I stop talking backwards, and tell you all you need to know? See, I've wanted you for years, and thought about you through the days. Imagined every way to bend you, and leave you feeling just amazed. But it seems as if the weeks, have dwindled down to hours. Yet we've still gained eternity, inside this bed of ours. 'Cause in my imagined nation, you've been ruling for some time. And your grace has struck me silent, like some phantom pantomime. And if there's a wall between us, I best prepare to climb. 'Cause all I needed was a reason, to do away with rhyme. For words are pleasing to the ear, but they seldom leave a mark. Unless they're laced with threats, that bite far worse than they bark. But there's no violence here, leaving plenty room for sex. Mixed with a touch of profanity, and our hands around each other's necks. As you look me in the eyes, and beg me not to stop. I know that inside the hourglass, a million grains have dropped. While I'm rocking back and forth, and moving steady like the tide. Just to delight the warmest shore, that I have ever been inside. 'Cause see, I've wanted you for years, and thought about you through the days. Imagined every way to bend you, and leave you feeling just amazed. But it seems as if the weeks, have dwindled down to hours. Yet we've still gained eternity, inside this bed of ours. 'Cause in my imagined nation, you've been ruling for some time. And your grace has struck me silent, like some phantom pantomime. And if there's a wall between us, I best prepare to climb. 'Cause all I needed was a reason, to do away with rhyme. And now I've rolled you on your side, so I can get a better view. Of each expression that you wear, as you enjoy each thing I do. And we're capsized in the sheets, like our sea has donned a veil. Hoping we could resurrect a love, as I slowly drive this final nail. But we're both powerless to fight, this every urge we have. While leaving marks upon our skin, and sharing moans and then a laugh. Wondering how we ever went so long, without reaching current heights. As we tolerated solitude, for what seemed like endless nights. But still I've wanted you for years, and thought about you through the days. Imagined every way to bend you, and leave you feeling just amazed. But it seems as if the weeks, have dwindled down to hours. Yet we've still gained eternity, inside this bed of ours. 'Cause in my imagined nation, you've been ruling for some time. And your grace has struck me silent, like some phantom pantomime. And if there's a wall between us, I best prepare to climb. 'Cause all I needed was a reason, to do away with rhyme. Girl, if my imagination was a place, folks could visit now and then. They would surely see your face, on the monuments within. And every portrait that was framed, would have value not a price. And they would surely bare your name, in A Fashion That's Precise. But I wonder if you'd call for God, with your hair inside my hand. Or if I grabbed the flesh upon your hips, as hard as you could stand. Before thrusting into you, with love and hate combined. And I wonder if the name upon your breath, would sound a lot like mine. 'Cause I've waited here for years, and thought about you through the days. Imagined every way to bend you, and leave you feeling just amazed. But it seems as if the weeks, have dwindled down to hours. Yet we've still gained eternity, inside this bed of ours. 'Cause in my imagined nation, you've been ruling for some time. And your grace has struck me silent, like some phantom pantomime. And if there's a wall between us, I best prepare to climb. 'Cause all I needed was a reason, to do away with rhyme...

A DEBT PAID IN INK

The Sweetest Sound

Desperation's setting in, like concrete drying ever still. And there's a hole inside of me, that I have tried to fill. But instead I have built a home, deep inside the crevices. As if I'd like to prove, that my inner Hell is Heaven-less. But tell me, what's the use of prayer, if nobody's listening. And what's the use of shining bright, if everybody's glistening. And it's this sweet futility, that wakes me from a nightly sleep. And though this life is killing me, my sanity is what I'll fight to keep. And there are times I think, that I am on the brink. But then I'll look around, and I'll hear the sweetest sound. Children laughing as they play, can always seem to make the day. Better than the previous, so thank you world, I've needed this. Now depression's setting in, like a black cloud overhead. Whispering things inside my ear, horrors better left unsaid. But instead they're ringing loud, and they echo on for days. This should not be allowed, but their persistence is worth some praise. But tell me, what's the use of prayer, if nobody's listening. And what's the use of shining bright, if everybody's glistening. And it's this sweet futility, that wakes me from a nightly sleep. And though this life is killing me, my sanity is what I'll fight to keep. And there are times I think, that I am on the brink. But then I'll look around, and I'll hear the sweetest sound. Children laughing as they play, can always seem to make the day. Better than the previous, so thank you world, I've needed this. And now I've got this funny feeling, that I haven't felt in years. I'll confess, it's got me reeling, thinking have I escaped my fears. Or is this just my mind, playing vicious tricks again? Or have I come to find, all the the things I've held within? Is determination creeping in? In hopes of clearing out the haze? Or is this act wearing thin? Like the sand beneath the waves? Answers escape my reach, leaving questions here abound. Yet I know inside my soul, that I've grown tired of the ground. So I should start standing up, and brush the dirt off of my clothes. Put the pieces back together, to see how the bigger picture goes. Or maybe take a few paces back, to the starting point of this. To get the point of view I've lacked, and see what I could have missed. But tell me, what's the use of life, if I'm scared of living it? And I don't have to have it all, to continue my giving it. And it's that sweet serenity, that's worth waking up to seek. And though this life was killing me, I have learned things are far from bleak…

A DEBT PAID IN INK

Lightning In A Bottle

They say that way too close is still too far, when it's compared to where you are. And I'm a patient man, who's waiting still. But how much time, will I have to kill? 'Til I can part my eyes, and see your face, shine the way it used to do. When we shared a bed, inside a space, and I slowly entered you. But in just a flash, I felt my passions crash. And I don't know why I feel this way again. But I'll gladly burn, until I feel my light return. To here and now and the bottle I'll catch it in. They say that losing love, still beats the feel of not feeling love at all. But that statement's false, and far from real, so don't ask a flying man to fall. I'll kiss the clouds, with waiting lips, hoping to find your face in there. But in case I don't, you should know, that your love's far beyond compare. But in just a flash, I felt my passions crash. And I don't know why I feel this way again. But I'll gladly burn, until I feel my light return. To here and now and the bottle I'll catch it in. Here I stand, a smiling fool, raising arms with glass in hand. Hoping that, some sacred rule, is what my lightning understands. They say that what you love, must be released into the waiting wild. In the hopes it will return, after you had to wait a while. But in just a flash, I felt my passions crash. And I don't know why I feel this way again. But I'll gladly burn, until I feel my light return. To here and now and the bottle I'll catch it in. So now here I stand, a smiling fool. With glass in hand, and cork in place. Thankful for, some sacred rule, that etched this smile upon my face. Because the one I loved, was once released, in to that waiting wild. And would you know, she did return, so I could love her all the while... Isn't that something?

CLYDE HURLSTON

This Thinking Man's A Fool

There are days I sleep too much. but those are days I need my rest. And there are days I feel the rush, of a heart that beats inside my chest. And there are days I'll call your name, but then some days I'll send a text. And there are days when I'm ashamed, of finding out what I'll do next. But these mistakes I make, prove perfection is a myth. 'Cause I'll be Jedi on some days, and on others you'll paint me Sith. But dear that doesn't mean, that I lack humility. No, to me it only means, that we can share a laugh at silly me. 'Cause I'll wear the darkest shades, so you can't see my eyes. When I'm staring at your parts, in a way that you'd despise. And I'll wear my heart upon a sleeve, as if instructed by the rules. 'Cause it's too hard to play it cool, when this thinking man is such a fool. There are days the sky is blue, and there are days I see only black. Then other days I'm seeing red, and patience's the virtue that I lack. But there are days when I'm laid bare, and the universe brings only pain. And days when thunderstorms can't compare, to the hurricanes inside my brain. Oh, these mistakes I make, prove perfection is a myth. 'Cause I'll be Jedi on some days, and on others you'll paint me Sith. But dear that doesn't mean, that I lack humility. No, to me it only means, that we can share a laugh at silly me. 'Cause I'll wear the largest shirts, to try and hide my flaws. And then I'll often read too much, inside each sentence paused. But I wear my heart upon a sleeve, as if instructed by the rules. 'Cause it's too hard to play it cool, when this thinking man is such a fool. There are days when I think too much, and yes this is one of them. And it's become a harder fact to face, it's why my outlook's so damn grim. But I'm not always gloom and doom, no, I have my better days. Like the times that you're inside my room, and you had me count the ways. That I could undress the sacred parts, seen from behind my darkened shades. While hoping when I'd lift my shirt, your attraction wouldn't fade. 'Cause you can lead a horse to water, but that won't make it drink. And you could tell me that you love me, but my mind will always think. That you're just being nice, until I give you what you want. And then I'll have to watch you leave, while saying "goodbye" as a taunt. And you'd rip that heart off its' sleeve, probably place it in your purse. Acting like it's a lovely parting gift, and a thinking man's foolish curse. But these mistakes I make, prove perfection is a myth. 'Cause I'll be Jedi on some days, and on others you'll paint me Sith. But dear that doesn't mean, that I lack humility. No, to me it only means, that we can share a laugh at silly me. 'Cause I'll wear the largest shirts, to try and hide my flaws. And then I'll often read too much, inside each sentence paused. But I wear my heart upon a sleeve, as if instructed by the rules. 'Cause it's too hard to play it cool, when this thinking man is such a fool. Love, won't you say a word to me, that'll make me feel alright? Or will this perception truly be, mine for a long and endless night? 'Cause I'd rather see a day, when someone took my fears away. And the monsters in my head, were either silent for left for dead. And I believe your kiss is powerful, but I haven't felt it heal. The shattered image behind the eyes, that only I can recognize. And this mirror is not to blame, I've slowly learned that fact. It's just years and years of loneliness, have left me here devoid of tact. And there are times truth be told, where you will think me cold. But dear, please know that this is true. This thinking man is a fool, but he'll only be a fool for you...

A DEBT PAID IN INK

The Overlooked Abyss

Is my head the labyrinth, they made so long ago? 'Cause I've been down so long, that my up won't seem to go. Resume its' rightful place, amongst the brightest lights. So now I'm sitting here, still wasting precious nights. But I have a reason to believe, that I will see the dawn. 'Cause not every night is endless, no, the darkness can't go on. And a soul may come with love, and arms still open wide. But she'll have to watch her step, if she ever gets inside. 'Cause I'll take her to the edge, of the overlooked abyss. Yeah, I've thought myself alive, but I've never felt like this. And yet I'm slightly terrified, that you may have a clue. Since the key to my salvation, still beats inside of you. But my mind has become a maze, that has a twist for every turn. And the air is filled with haze, from the bridges left to burn. And yet it's still easier to see, that my intentions are unclear. And every possibility, still suffocates with fear. Thinking that a sure oblivion, lurks in the darkness down below. But after so many years eclipsed, how could hope begin to grow? When this once fertile ground, was poisoned to the core. By lies I've told myself, like, "I don't deserve much more." Still I have a reason to believe, that I will see the dawn. 'Cause not every night is endless, no, the darkness can't go on. And a soul may come with love, and arms still open wide. But she'll have to watch her step, if she ever gets inside. 'Cause I'll take her to the edge, of the overlooked abyss. Yeah, I've thought myself alive, but I've never felt like this. And yet I'm slightly terrified, that you may have a clue. Since the key to my salvation, still beats inside of you. Yet beyond each precipice, lies a solid ground in reach. While my growing discontent, lies like oil upon a beach. And within that blackened sand, lies each precious grain I've lost. While trying to count the ways, I've deserved to pay the cost. For the darkness in my eyes, that wants to suffocate the light. While knowing if it did, this fool would be proven right. I'd rather dodge that route, and find another way. To ignite the hope within my veins, and shine throughout the day. Because I once read a quote, that stuck inside my mind. And then I quickly added on, bits of wisdom that I'd find. He said, "I burn with life, I love, slay, and I'm content." And it was after reading this, I wondered where my passion went. Had I become such a lonely man, that I would shun the sun? And would my heart burn with hate, that I held tight for everyone? Where was my lust for life? And a woman's sweet embrace? Where was the joy derived, from her lips with every taste? Where was my inner god that aimed to conquer flesh? While drowned in ego's bliss, and proclaimed myself her best? Using my manly hands as eyes, it's her every curve I'd read. As she climbed on top of me, and rode her bare, majestic steed. While climbing up to every peak, we've ever reached before. Lost inside a mental fog, described in erotic books of 'lore. As if learned sweet tantra's art, or felt the kama sutra's grace. Oh, where is the darling girl, that will bring this about with haste? 'Cause she'll be the reason to believe, that I will see the dawn. For not every night is endless, and the darkness can't go on. Dear, have you come with love, and your legs open wide? 'Cause I've longed to watch your eyes, as I slowly went inside. Hoping to take you to the edge, of the overlooked abyss. 'Cause

I've thought myself alive, but I've never felt like this. And yet I'm slightly terrified, that you may have a clue. About this growing list of things, that I'd die to do to you...

CLYDE HURLSTON

A King Within My Skin

I've learned that castles in the sand, are the minions of the tide. And what I'll never understand, are the opinions some provide. But it's from here on out, that I will only listen to. Words distilled from lies, and placed in statements true. 'Cause I've faced the consequence, of an all consuming doubt. And this new found confidence, has helped me tune it out. 'Cause my will has turned to armor, forged inside the flame. And my wants are now demands, so you all must bare some blame. Oh, my sword is made of flesh, made to please my chosen queen. And my throne's inside my bones, so let me tell you what I mean. There's a king within my skin, that's now begun to rule. Without a need for counsel, he's grown too wise for fools. And this king within my skin, would never hide behind a shield. 'Cause the world is on his shoulders, so he can't afford to yield. I've learned the weak will moderate, and fools will just consume. But he who rules himself, can always stop and then resume. And yes, the brave are dying young, and the timid dying slow. But I have far too much to see, to not know which way to go. So I've taken doubt by storm, and pushed it to the ledge. 'Cause I'm fed up with the norm, so I pushed it off the edge. And I've come to find the view, is better standing tall. 'Cause hanging your head down, will make it easier to fall. But now my will has turned to armor, forged inside the flame. And my wants are now demands, so you all must bare some blame. Oh, my sword is made of flesh, and made to please my queen. And my throne's inside my bones, so let me tell you what I mean.

A DEBT PAID IN INK

There's a king within my skin, that's now begun to rule. Without a need for counsel, he's grown too wise for fools. And this king within my skin, would never hide behind a shield. 'Cause the world is on his shoulders, so he can't afford to yield. Yeah, it's hard to see this crown, that often feels like thorns. Knowing all men have a devil, within them hiding horns. But pitchforks have no use, when your enemy is seen. In mirrors once seduced, by reflections far from clean. But behind these castle walls, are the emptiest of halls. For the ravens bring no words, and the phones they bring no calls. So maybe silence has been sown, in the fields I used to plow. While hoping I would be shown, the way beyond the here and now. And if I found that path, I'd wipe the sweat from off my brow. And fight to blaze a trail, that would illuminate the ground. And now my will has turned to armor, forged inside that flame. And my wants are now demands, so you all must bare some blame. Oh, my sword is made of flesh, made to please my chosen queen. And my throne's inside my bones, so let me tell you what I mean. There's a king within my skin, that's now begun to rule. Without a need for counsel, he's grown too wise for fools. And this king within my skin, would never hide behind a shield. 'Cause the world is on his shoulders, so he can't afford to yield. I watch my castle kiss the clouds, as it's held by pillars made of stone. Knowing the world I choose to rule, will only be my own. And the moat the flows around, seeks to remind me of. The water I used to tread, when this world denied me love. But in time they've come around, and they seek to be the ones. Around the fabled table round, to get their hands on all the crumbs. But my circle's stayed the size, that it always used to be. So as I conquer more than doubts, my knights will be right next to me. 'Cause my will has turned to armor, forged inside the flame. And my wants are now demands, so you all must bare some blame. Oh, my sword is made of flesh, made to please my chosen queen. And my throne's inside my bones, so let me tell you what I mean. There's a king within my skin, that's now begun to rule. Without a need for counsel, for he's grown too wise for fools. And this king within my skin, would never hide behind a shield. 'Cause the world is on his shoulders, so he can't afford to yield. And now that I have found, what I thought forever lost. You should know that sound, is the preparing of a dish best served with frost. And my friend, I've paid the price, for being far too nice. But I will follow my own advice, and make sure that I avoid being the next one on a cross…

A DEBT PAID IN INK

A Fire Burning Bright

I found the spark inside a match, after it was struck on this. Humble square in hand, held so tightly I could miss. This fleeting chance I have, to set this world alight. 'Cause the smell of gasoline, means I'll show them all tonight. That the ones you throw away, will come around someday. And illuminate your night, with a fire burning bright. And while you're blinded by the shine, I think you'll come to find. That the ones you do forsake, will leave your ashes in their wake. So you can look and count the stars, then start including me. Because I finally found a way, to catch the things eluding me. And the growing self-respect, that I once held in check. Has now bloomed into the noose, I'll slip around your neck. 'Cause the ones you throw away, will come around someday. And illuminate your night, with a fire burning bright. And while you're blinded by the shine, I think you'll come to find. That the ones you do forsake, will leave your ashes in their wake. So if you ever feel knocked down, just confuse them with a laugh. As you start to shake the ground, then crack it all in half. And as they start to run, they'll see you're far from done. Then they'll have to realize, the raging fire in your eyes. 'Cause there's a phoenix in us all, hiding just behind our skin. Waiting 'til the day we fall, to rise back up again. And start screaming at a world, that turned its' back on us. So when our flaming wings unfurl, we will turn them all to dust. 'Cause the ones you throw away, will come around someday. And illuminate your night, with a fire burning bright. And while you're blinded by the shine, I think you'll come to find. That the ones you do forsake, will leave your ashes in their wake. So let them scream and beg, as we take them down a peg. And show them all the view, once shared by me and you. Then they'll have to see, just how it feels to be. Stepped and frowned upon, until the day is gone. And as it turns to night, know we will be alright. For the flames will keep us warm, and keep us free from harm. 'Cause the ones they threw away, have come around today. To set aflame the night, with a fire burning bright. And now they're blinded by the shine, and I think they've come to find. That the ones they did forsake, have left the ashes of the past, lying in their wake...

A DEBT PAID IN INK

The Price Of Denial

Take another aching step, that takes you through uncharted land. Observe your surroundings dear, until you start to understand. The images your eyes will see, are those better parts of me. And it is because of you, that these better parts are now in view. But here you'll find the water's cold, like the shoulders I received. There were things I said to you, but they were not believed. So I want your eyes to see, as your mistakes are now displayed. Still it's you I long to lay beside, in this bed you never made. Take another lasting view, see your face upon the walls. And my voice it echoes true, hear the sounds of my unheeded calls. When I cried out late at night, after the day had not gone right. But I searched and you went unfound, so now you roam this unforgiving ground. And it's here you'll find the water's cold, like the shoulders I received. There were things I said to you, but they were not believed. So I want your eyes to see, as your mistakes are now displayed. Still it's you I long to lay beside, in this bed you never made. Take a breather now my dear, feel the breath consumed by lungs. Jacob's ladder lies in sight, feel free to use its' waiting rungs. To escape this vengeful mind of mine, that grew obsessions slowly over time. And it wants you to long reside, within the confines of the one you denied. Here where you'll find the water's cold, like the shoulders I received. There were things I said to you, but they were not believed. So I want your eyes to see, as your mistakes are now displayed. Still it's you I long to lay beside, in this bed you never made. You will find no tribulations here, but you will receive a little trial. To see if you can afford to pay, the price of your denial. And I would take installments dear, if you plan to reimburse that way. But the thing I truly want, is to find a way to make you stay…With me.

A DEBT PAID IN INK

The Confines Of A Pantomime

When you start to analyze, do you find your hidden prize? Beneath the layers of the veil, that we cling to like a sail. As we float adrift and tireless, until we feel how close the fire is. To our fragile little shell of skin, that protects everything we've kept within. The confines of a pantomime, that will find its' fair release in time. But until you start to speak it out, you'll only know what fear's about. And shutting down a point of view, will cause the world to point at you. While crying of your heresy, since they're so blind they'll never see. That when you to start to look around, you can describe the thing you found. That has caused your eyes to turn away, from all of this ignorance today. Like blaming ills on darkened hues, while counting every cent they lose. That's not inside their collection plates, while scientists discuss our final fates. Inside the confines of a pantomime, that will find its' fair release in time. But until you start to speak it out, you'll only know what fear's about. And shutting down a point of view, will cause the world to point at you. While crying of your heresy, since they're so blind they'll never see. That we could paint our faces white, but it won't make the silence right. And pretending we are trapped inside, a see-through box just may provide. The excuse so many need, to not allow their souls to feed. On the answers that we're searching for, so in the end they just confuse us more...

CLYDE HURLSTON

A Reflex I've Gained

I stare at the glass, see shades of the past. And I wonder, "is God disappointed in me?" 'Cause my bitterness, has bled into pride. And now rage has joined them in me. This destruction I've wrought, is not conscious thought. No, it's just a reflex I've gained. And the lines on my face, show time that I waste. Revealing each shade of my shame. So peel me away, from all that I am. And show me whatever remains. Then tell God and his son, that I'm far from done. But it's hard to call out their names. Oh, what I need from you, is just to be true. Save your pity for someone in need. 'Cause I've buried my hopes, along with my cares. And no, I'm not proud of that deed. But I feel that it's best, to lay them to rest. 'Cause they've only blessed me with tears. And now my wasted youth, is a sign that the truth. Was on the list of my greatest fears. So peel me away, from all that I am. And show me whatever remains. Then tell God and his son, that I'm far from done. But it's hard to call out their names. I wish I could stay, but I should go away. It seems I'm best when I am alone. So don't bother to ring, I've said everything. You don't need to reach for your phone. And I hate that I feel, like my thoughts are real. But they're the only voice that I've heard. And you may disagree, but darling to me. There's some truth in each little word. See, each wall that I've built, the mortar is guilt. For feeling the way that I do. 'Cause someone out there, is in true despair. And not they're not here crying to you. I'm so worthless my dear, you don't have to fear. I won't waste anymore of your time. Though the seasons may change, my outlook is strange. But there's a reason behind every rhyme. So peel me away, from all that I am. And show me whatever remains. Then tell God and his son, that I'm far from done. But it's hard to call out their names. 'Cause I really don't know, if I still believe. Or if I ever did at all...

CLYDE HURLSTON

The Only Option Is War

From atop this humble hill, I see the sides as they are drawn. Like a line inside the sand, as the moon gives way to dawn. Now flags are trapped inside a breeze, waiting for soldiers to bring. The much needed munitions, that will help these cannons sing. 'Cause when all the talk has died, and they've attacked your pride. Oh, I've said it all before, the only option is war. Raise your sword or loaded gun, then you'll be the quoted one. Instead of getting to see, how painful surrender can be. 'Cause the spoils go the victor, and if you would have picked her. I feel that you wouldn't be, the one down on bended knee. And the lessons that you're learning, will continue their burning. As you slowly realize, you lost your grip upon a prize. 'Cause when all the talk has died, and they've attacked your pride. Oh, I've said it all before, the only option is war. Raise your sword or loaded gun, then you'll be the quoted one. Instead of getting to see, how painful surrender can be. I've heard every story friend, I've seen her spill her every tear. And though wits were at their end, she still wished to hold you near. So she was often called a fool, by myself and those who cared. 'Cause when it came love, it seems like pain was all you shared. 'Cause when all the talk has died, and they've attacked your pride. Oh, I've said it all before, the only option is war. Raise your sword or loaded gun, then you'll be the quoted one. Instead of getting to see, how painful surrender can be. And I'd rather see a queen alone, than to see her sit beside your throne. For truly heavy is your head, and no truer words were ever said. Because jesters often wear the crown, when there is no one else around. Who can put up a greater fight, well my friend, that changes tonight. 'Cause now all the talk has died, and you've been attacking her pride. So, I've said this shit before, the only option is war. Now I raise my pen like a loaded gun, until I'll be the quoted one. And you'll be getting to see, that she looks much better with me. Here atop this humble hill, we see your side has withdrawn. And now her lovely hand, fights to hide as she yawns. As your white flag's trapped inside a breeze, and waiting for soldiers to bring. Your pride a much needed doctor, that will help ease the sting...

CLYDE HURLSTON

A Hope In Need Of Repair

A friend once said to me, "There is a sadness in your eyes. And it's as if the only thing you ever see, is beauty when it dies. But there must be more to this look, than the bad days in your past. 'Cause it's as if you do believe, that they will forever last. And friend, I have no other choice, but to loudly disagree. 'Cause I have seen with my own eyes, just how great a life can be. So I hope you'll finally see an end, to the black clouds overhead. Otherwise they'll slowly sap, your happiness instead. And the you I used to know, would share his laughter and a smile. But from the look upon your face, I can tell it's been awhile. Since you ever thought of me, and the times we used to share. And you've grown colder to the touch, 'cause you think no one has ever cared. But again I'll have to disagree, though I only speak for self. 'Cause there's nothing more I'd rather see, than an improvement to your health. And I do refer to every kind, not just the obvious. 'Cause honestly it wasn't far, that your old way's gotten us. So you should try another way, to see a change inside your life. Instead of living as a monument, and testament to strife. 'Cause I know there's many things, for which you're capable to do. You'd only have to want to start, and use resolve to see it through. But it seems you'd be content, to just rest in the same old place. And have your current bitterness, stay and leave the same old taste. It's like your mind's a barren land, where pride it does decay. And yet the seeds of doubting things, are still growing well today. And friend, I don't believe in blaming God, for your current, wretched state.

Instead I pray you will see the way, and He'll help to clean your slate. But if you need some more advice, or if you need to see a smile. You should feel free to call, and I'll make it worth your while. But until that day finally comes, please try to take a little care. Because the way it sounds to me, that your hope just needs repair. And know you're not the only one, to feel like their hurt is justified. It's just, the Clyde that I once knew, well, he must have died. ...And I miss him dearly."

CLYDE HURLSTON

If There Is Such A Thing

As each new day is born, my self-confidence is worn. Like a tattered sail that's been displayed, through a battle torn and frayed. But there are days when skies are clear, and they occur this time of year. But when your skies are often gray, you're not left with much to say. So you try to think the thoughts, that could inspire just a smile. But that wish is all for naught, in this world so cold and vile, 'cause... If there's such a thing as grace, I have never seen it's face. And if there's such a thing as pride, I know that mine has died. And if there's such a thing as fate, I've discovered it too late. But if there's way I could restart, I'd want it with all my heart. If there is such a thing... As each new day grows old, a thousand lies are likely told. By both your friends and foes alike, oh, the graph would show a spike. But no, things aren't always bad, and there are good times to be had. But they are things that often miss, when aiming at a wretched soul like this. So you could try to think the thoughts, that could inspire just a smile. But that wish is all for naught, in this world so cold and vile, 'cause... If there's such a thing as grace, I have never seen it's face. And if there's such a thing as pride, I know that mine has died. And if there's such a thing as fate, I've discovered it too late. But if there's way I could restart, I'd want it with all my heart. 'Cause she gave me glimpses of her grace, and it seems I spat into her face. And it truly wounded all her pride, so now the flame inside has died. And that's the expected form of fate, when you apologize too late. But if there's way I could restart, I'd want it with all my heart. And as each new night is born, my scarlet letter's proudly worn. For I betrayed her with my words, and became the handsome scourge. That was lashing out in print, as each letter made its' dent. In the designer armor that she wore, that was tailored just before. She ever had an urge to love, the fool who just couldn't rise above. The hate he had for self, that was flaunted like it's wealth. But in the end the fool was broke, and with every angry word he spoke. His prize would drift away, so now it's through the ashes of bridges burned that he must sift before he'll say... Oh, you could try to think the thoughts, that could inspire just a smile. But that wish is all for naught, in this world so cold and vile, 'cause... If there's such a thing as grace, I have never seen it's face. And if there's such a thing as pride, I know that mine has died. And if there's such a thing as fate, I've discovered it too late. But if there's way I could restart, I'd want it with all my heart. 'Cause she gave me glimpses of her grace, and it seems I spat into her face. And it truly wounded all her pride, so now the flame inside has died. And that's the expected form of fate, when you apologize too late. But if there's way I could restart, I'd want it with all my heart. Oh, if there's a way I could restart, I'd want her and only her. And I'd want her with all of my damaged heart. But that's only if there is such a thing, inside my chest....

CLYDE HURLSTON

The Death Of All That's Fair

I've ventured far and often wide, to see the things I've been denied. But here inside your darling room, I sense discontent is now in bloom. For you hate your place upon the top, of the pedestal from which you've dropped. Your sense of self-respect below, hoping it wouldn't make a sound or show. That the things I see can't be unseen, but that doesn't mean we can't come clean. And say the things we want to say, before they take our voice away. So darling scream until your lungs, use every single breath of air. And I will be awake and waiting here, to mourn the death of all that's fair. I've ventured far and far too close, to find the things nobody knows. Like a moth with eyes on pretty flames, I fell victim to their petty games. Yet here I stand so tall and resolute, with my own horn to proudly toot. But I'd much prefer to share with you, if you could bare a better point of view. 'Cause the things I see can't be unseen, but that doesn't mean we can't come clean. And say the things we want to say, before they take our voice away. So darling scream until your lungs, use every single breath of air. And I will be awake and waiting here, to mourn the death of all that's fair. Then darling scream until you see, the way things were, supposed to be. It's then you'll see their lack of care, for all that's just and just a little fair. They'd much prefer to tilt the odds, until they greet the greener gods. That they fold and often place upon, the pedestal from which you've gone. Away in search of calmer tides, that a change of scenery provides. But me, I'll just stay here and wait, as this world becomes a cleaner slate. Whether it be the waves or shining sun, Mother will get rid of everyone. Then maybe I will sit atop the ash...

Post-It Notes

Everyday I feel my decency erode.
Trying in vain to find the strength
I need, To keep up this mask of civility.
But often I stumble; and as my patience
evaporates, Any remaining tact is
expelled in my exhales.
Tyler warned me years ago,
That predators could pose as
house pets. But I didn't listen. Instead
I charged forward as a fool.
Fighting the good fight,
Whilst simultaneously digging
To mine the goodness out of everyone.
Living like some naive hero who has
seen nothing, If not through the eyes
of hope. Yet in secret, still aching internally,
Like a dying martyr who has felt everything,
Except the acceptance of fate.
Why must some lessons be learned
with pain? Why must the heads hardened
by pride, be joined in matrimony with
the most tender of hides?
I guess it was true when I once said,
That scars are better reminders
than post-it notes.

CLYDE HURLSTON

Apocalyptic Disappointment

It seems I have indeed awaken, having rose before the sun. But I had a feeling that this day, would be like any other one. For the sky was just a little dark, but bloomed into the brightest shade. Of blue that there has ever been, and I have witnessed it displayed. But there was a lot of chatter, on the little glowing screen. About impending cataclysms, and things they have foreseen. But for every false prediction, I have cracked a smile. And for every prophecy, my laughter went the extra mile. 'Cause we're so very eager, to wait and see the bitter end. That we'll follow any seller, who's masquerading as a friend. But it seems I have indeed awaken, and I'm counting every cloud. That will surely dissipate, with every prayer that's said aloud. But they're recounted by the ones, who believed the ancient texts. And were getting things in order, since they knew what was coming next. And they engaged in a lot of chatter, on the little glowing screen. About impending cataclysms, and things they have foreseen. But for every false prediction, I have cracked a smile. And for every prophecy, my laughter went the extra mile. 'Cause we're so very eager, to wait and see the bitter end. That we'll follow any seller, who's masquerading as a friend. But girl, it's time to look beyond the veil, 'cause there's more than what you see. And now my mind is sitting sail, to where it is supposed to be. And with some patience I will raise, the anchors from the floor. And I'd shower you with praise, for now and evermore. And this man would gladly sing, if the words would sound as pure. As they did upon your lips, when you said that I'll endure. This apocalypse at hand, when

A DEBT PAID IN INK

I'm losing sight of land. Trying not to drown inside a sea, that killed who I've tried to be. Or will another savior rise, to pull me out of this? Not knowing that here before my eyes, I've seen the death of bliss. Caused by the cavalcade of chatter, on the little glowing screen. About impending cataclysms, and things they have foreseen. But for every false prediction, I have cracked a smile. And for every prophecy, my laughter went the extra mile. 'Cause we're so very eager, to wait and see the bitter end. That we'll follow any seller, who's masquerading as a friend. But if we took time to look beyond the wall, we'd see horizons start to blur. 'Cause Mother Nature wants revenge, for all we've done to her. And there's no fool among us now, who could ever disagree. And say we don't deserve, all that's come to be. But now this man will gladly sing, hoping the words will sound as pure. As they did upon your lips, when I say we will find a cure. For our sense of disappointment, since the end was not at hand. And we never drowned inside a sea, nor ever lost our sight of land. But maybe another generation, will still have room to rise. And one day pull us out of this, as I fight the tears inside my eyes. Knowing the world could have ended, and you would've left me here alone. Because you were far too busy, making sure the world's attention was your own. By simply adding to the chatter, on the little glowing screen. About the latest cataclysm, you were too blind to have foreseen.
But for your every false prediction, I have cracked a smile. And for your every prophecy, my laughter went the extra mile. 'Cause you were so very eager, to say your new love would never end. That you followed the latest seller, who was masquerading as a friend. And

CLYDE HURLSTON

how did that work out for you?

A DEBT PAID IN INK

The Devil On My Shoulder Said

I've watched you kill your self-respect, each time and time again. And I've watched you mutilate, any pride you've held within. And that's all fine and well, but friend, what I have to know. Is why you'll wait 'til now, to try and get the stones to show. That you'll try to find a brighter day, and you'll hope to find it right away. Because I'll just get to watch you fail, and have a darker tale to tell. 'Cause it's when you don't prevail, that you go back inside the well. Just to drown in the despair, that feels so much like home. Oh, the devil on my shoulder said, that I will spend my life alone. And I've watched you as you wait, for her to look your way. Thinking every single time, that this might be your day. But friend, she'll never waste her time, on a soul who looks like you. 'Cause you're far too fat to miss, and far too hideous to kiss. So you can try to find a brighter day, but you'll never find it right away. And then I'll get to watch you fail, and have a darker tale to tell. 'Cause it's when you don't prevail, that you go back inside the well. Just to drown in the despair, that feels so much like home. Oh, the devil on my shoulder said, that I will spend my life alone. And I've watched you question God, like you were a friend of mine. But your loyalty is flawed, 'cause you crawl back to Him in time. But I will seek to own your heart, and I'll prove His lack of care. 'Cause you've often cried and prayed, and tell me, was He ever there? Friend, I know your answer's no, it doesn't have to leave your lips. He's placed everything you'd want, far beyond your fingertips. And He will tempt you with the girl, who liked you as a child. But now that you're adults, you can barely see her smile. Unless it's at another man, who'll treat her worse than you. So if you really want to change, friend, this is what you have to do. Accept that you'll never find a brighter day, and you have to accept it right away. And then I'll get to watch Him fail, as I enjoy the darker tale you'll tell. 'Cause it's when He don't prevail, that even Heaven feels like Hell. And then these darling flames, start to feel so much like home. Oh, the devil on my shoulder said, that I will spend eternity alone. And friend, I fear he's right, because when I look around. Everything resembles night, and there is no light around. And the things I once held dear, just don't feel the same. And I know you'd hate to hear, just who I'd like to blame. Because it's not my God, I point the finger at myself. And yes, my point of view is flawed, I finally agree with someone else. But I just can't help the hate, that I've always had for me. And so now it's here I'll wait, as things get bad for me. Because it's how they always were, for as long I'll recall. And pass this message on to her, "just know you're not to blame at all." Because I've accepted there is no brighter day, since this world took my fight away. And then it got to watch me fail, and it heard the darker tale I'd tell. 'Cause it's when I don't prevail, that I go back inside the well. Just to drown in the despair, that feels so much like home. Oh, the devil on my shoulder said, that I will spend eternity alone. And despite what everyone says, he was right.

A DEBT PAID IN INK

The Devil Gets To Boast

He was standing atop the rubble, his eyes asked the only survivor near. "Tell me, where's your precious God," and I lent my silence to his ear. But he must have had a second sense, or could've smelled my suffering. That he would arrive with false pretense, and thought enough to ring. And call upon my wretched state, as if to smile and say hello. But instead, having motives all the while, to see how far my despair may go. So this handsome man, draped in white, chose to clear his throat and speak. And condescension wrapped his tongue, as he asked, "must your mood remain so bleak?" And I shook my head while fighting tears, looking at the pieces of my life. While he stooped down to inspect a piece, that was sharper than any fabled knife. And this referenced piece was double-edged, and labeled "curiosity". Which he then skipped across the water's face, and watch sink with great velocity.
He said, "dear friend, if I can call you that, I've just removed a burden from your mind. For it's a trait that often killed the cat, as you humans have come to find. And you see that other guy, who they praise for sitting on a cloud? Well, he frowns upon that sort of thing, especially, if proudly said aloud. Just look at His first creations, whose crime was simply sharing fruit. And He condemned them for their actions, during their curious pursuit. See? He claims to make you in His image, and then gives you these desires. Hoping that you will prove me wrong, and escape my waiting fires. 'Cause we once made a wager, so very many moons ago. That He would give you all free will,

and then we'll see where you may go, And I believe
the way He has you wired, will only lead you all to
me. So that's why I encourage you, to be as indulgent
as you can be. Because I know it's in your natures,
the way that cells are in your bloods. And I'd never
tell just one to build a boat, while I killed the rest in
floods. And I noticed you shook your head, when the
word wager left my lips. As if it was a molten lie, that
left it's mark upon your fingertips. But I'll ask you
to call upon your memory, and think of dear Job's
brutal plight. 'Cause the things that I was allowed to
do, were just so He could prove that He was right.
So now I'm asking how much you will endure, just to
assuage a greater being's pride? While your inner
rage is growing pure, over the answers you have
been denied." And in my head his words did ring,
but he's still the Devil after all. And though he's not
in serpent form, I know he still seeks to see me fall.
Because it's when things are at their very worst,
and my cursing God is close. That the Devil feels
he's nearing first, and then he gets to boast. So now
he's here so full of self, and full of something I would
never say. Thinking that the card that's up his sleeve,
is simply all he has to play. And he said, "while it may
behoove us now, to sit and share a verbal joust. I will
offer you the greatest deal, since I brokered one with
Faust. See? He merely wanted knowledge, and the
power to catch the eye. Of some silly, human tart,
who didn't know he was alive. And in return I got his
soul, delivered by Mephistopheles to me. Despite
Heaven having now become, the one place he'd never
see. And are you a better man that he, showing
so pious of a stance? That here under this pale
moonlight, you still wouldn't share a dance? And I

said, "let me stop you there, for I'm beginning to hear enough. 'Cause you're just here to pick the bones, since the going's gotten rough. 'Cause you see, it's times like these, that I don't know what I should believe. But I find it quite insulting that, you think me easy to deceive. 'Cause while I want the smaller things, my pockets only cry for gold. And to me, that doesn't ever mean, I'll just buy anything I'm sold. Because you're standing here with a smirk, to feed me massive lies. Since you recognize I have some nagging doubts, that you intend to pacify. And Faust was a greater fool than I, for dealing with the Son of Dawn. And every other tale you'll tell today, I will have to greet it with a yawn. For I am here and not impressed, with any soul you may collect. And your sensing of my inner doubts, may indeed prove to be correct. But that doesn't mean I will ever sell, this soul I'm fighting to appease. And certainly not to catch the eye, of a girl who'd let me wither in the breeze. And while you're here I should prove a point, to those who claim to work for God. 'Cause their true faces seem to favor yours, and I think their points of views are flawed. And that doesn't make me a better soul, because I will admit my flaws. And I've grown tired of not feeling whole, I'm not here for your forced applause. So as long as I'm a human with free will, I believe that I will always sin. And while you may always get to boast, in the end, my friend, God will always win. That is... If I can call you that... " And as I walked away with pride, the Devil's eyes were locked on me. And throughout that time we shared a gaze, I saw the things that a man shouldn't ever be. But I overlooked the simple fact, that someone was looking down. And after I had walked out of view, he thought it was time to bless the ground. And then God came down the ladder that, Jacob had best described for us. And at first He wasn't going to intervene, But I guess He felt He must. Then he walked over to Lucifer and said, "Surely little Morning Star, you knew that young man's soul was mine. And yes, I could say I told you so, but let's save that for another time..."

A DEBT PAID IN INK

Illusions

It is pointless to resist.
So I just smile and nod along.
Pretending that I don't see what's
behind the curtain.
Allowing myself to get high,
Off the smoke and mirrors on display.
I keep buying these illusions,
That my heart wants to sell my mind.
Visions of happiness overdue.
Made to coincide with dreams
beginning to come true.
But in truth, those are just tall tales.
"I have no tree waiting for me."
All I want, all I deserve are in these
empty hands. For this is the really,
real world. Demons walk upright here.
They stand next to you,
And sometimes lie beside you.
And angels?
They weep in realms unseen.
Restrained and gagged.
And me?
I finally learned what John Milton meant.
"Abashed the Devil stood,
And felt how awful goodness is."
Because, the Devil must have known.
Heaven is just a dream.
And at dawn, we all shall be cast
out by the morning sun.
Back into the purgatory, we
know as being awake.

CLYDE HURLSTON
Suffocate The Flame

Has my change in disposition, left your feet on shaky ground? Have the echoes of assumptions, left you with a haunting sound? Have you felt an emptiness, for which I am now to blame? Or has there been a night, where you wished to scream my name? 'Cause beneath the arm that sealed you in, lies a place you'd go again. Where you were delighted slightly, thinking this should happen nightly. And I know that you've been wishing, for things I did not provide. So there's no need to wonder, why your feelings have been denied. You want to suffocate the flame, and hope it never burns. But you can't escape the heat, 'cause the body never learns. That you can't suffocate the flame, 'cause it will only rise. To the heights you've never seen, with your disgruntled eyes. Has withdrawal left you with it's symptoms, like a strong aversion to the fumes? You know, the kind that left us blind, and stumbling 'til our dance resumed? Baby, have I been your worst, or just the one you wish to love? Or am I the darkened magnet that you've failed to rise above? 'Cause beneath the arm that sealed you in, lies a place you'd go again. Where you were delighted slightly, thinking this should happen nightly. And I know that you've been wishing, for things I did not provide. So there's no need to wonder, why your feelings have been denied. You want to suffocate the flame, and hope it never burns. But you can't escape the heat, 'cause the body never learns. That you can't suffocate the flame, 'cause it will only rise. To the heights you've never seen, with your disgruntled eyes. Such a circumstantial silence, has filled the growing space. That's between the both of us, since we were last face to face. But that is more my fault, than it ever was your own. Since I've brought things to a halt, and left you all alone. But it's really for the best, if you're asking honestly. Because deep inside my chest, there's a hole within my soul. And no matter how I try, or how much I used to pray. There's a doubt inside of me, that won't ever go away. So baby, you should leave me, and go about your better days. And you will forget me with some time, then you can file me under, "phase." And then you can find a man, that spends more time loving you. Than hating on himself, and maybe he'll even have that good book on his shelf. Instead of lonely pictures, fit inside of broken frames. Shit, maybe when we're done, we'll forget each other's names. But that's another thing I doubt, since you were wonderful indeed. But now I will step aside, so you can find the affection that you need. 'Cause beneath the arm that sealed you in, lies a heart that barely beats. But it's trying to let its' anger go, hoping that it has some more to show. And I know that you've been wishing, for things I did not provide. So there's no need to wonder, why your feelings have been denied. You want to suffocate the flame, and hope it never burns. But you can't escape the heat, 'cause the body never learns. That you can't suffocate the flame, 'cause it will only rise. To the heights you've never seen, with your disgruntled eyes. But baby, if you blink, please don't picture me at all. Because I don't deserve your thoughts, nor do I deserve a call. So forget me for the best, or remember at your worst. But never stop your moving on, the steps get easier past the first. And if you find me in a glass of wine, be sure to drink me down. 'Cause things will go much smoother, if my reflection's not around. So don't let the coldness of a beer, remind you of me dear. Nor let a straight shot of something hard, force your pretty eyes to tear. 'Cause what is meant to be will be, but I think it for the best. If you just stayed away from me, 'cause all I seem to do is weigh you down...

A DEBT PAID IN INK
The Familiar Pull

Looks like another year is gone, and I'm lying in the same old place. The mirror's still fogging up, hoping to avoid the same old face. And truly, there's a bitterness, rising up inside my veins. But I don't want to be the man, that constantly complains. So maybe while I'm lying here, and hoping that my life will change. I could finally get off my ass, then moving on wouldn't feel so strange. But as my body starts to rise, I'm feeling that familiar pull. And I'm thinking that I had my fill, of seeing this glass any less than full. A heart displayed on my sleeve, will only find a way to bleed. While leading me to believe, inside I have all I'll ever need. It's time to walk into the sun, find a little room to shine. Knowing that I'm far from done, so I'll let this world know that it's mine. Friend, I used to think I had enough, but now I feel I need some more. I've spent my life behind these walls, and now I'm walking out that door. And out into this open world, so full of things I've yet to see. Past time to let these wings unfurl, and see how warm the sky can be. Tired of being on the ground, with this pair of angry knees. Taking things out on everyone, moods shifting like the breeze. See, first I'd be up then down, while looking for a way around. The advice I did receive, pretending I didn't hear the sound. But a heart displayed on my sleeve, will only find a way to bleed. While leading me to believe, inside I have all I'll ever need. It's time to walk into the sun, find a little room to shine. Knowing that I'm far from done, so I'll let this world know that it's mine. Spent so many minutes posturing, and acting like I know what's best.

But now I've got a lot of room, to get this shit up off my chest. Girl, I used to be so consumed, with all this hatred for you. That I could forget about my lust, and focus on what you put me through. And if you were right here, I wouldn't shed a damn tear. I'd simply ask you, "where the hell you've been?" 'Cause we both know that it ain't been near!" And a heart displayed on my sleeve, will only find a way to bleed. While leading me to believe, inside I have all I'll ever need. It's time to walk into the sun, find a little room to shine. Knowing that I'm far from done, so I'll let this world know that it's mine. And while I can't ignore the wrong I've done, I'm gonna focus on the right I'll do. And put my mind on much better things, and just ignore the sight of you. 'Cause I can't ignore the things I've said, while doubt was ringing in my head. But you were just a fantasy, that never came to share my bed. And I can't ignore mistakes I've made, as I danced along my faults displayed. But I will start anew this year, don't need to call a spade a spade. But there's something that I want to share, to the few people that always cared. If you give me just a little time, I'm hoping the bridges that I tried to burn, will finally be repaired. Because a heart displayed on my sleeve, will only find a way to bleed. While leading me to believe, inside I have all I'll ever need. It's time to walk into the sun, find a little room to shine. Knowing that I'm far from done, so I'll let this world know that it's mine. In closing on this brighter day, there's a final thing that I have to say. If you start feeling a familiar pull, you should know that it could be me, reclaiming all of those that I once pushed away...

Intimate With Hell

Please don't speak to me of life.
Not even on my best days.
Know for certain, that I have no
patience for your gods. For I have
seen only devils in the flesh. And
I'd rather continue suffering in silence,
than to kneel and play the pleasant
pantomime. Look deep within my tired,
brown eyes and see that I have known hell
without burning. And even sadder yet,
I have seen the dissolution of dreams.
So save your forced compliments,
And your feigned concern.
Because I would rather drown in honest
indifference, than to wade and tread
your water when it's trite.
The things I have wanted most in life,
have been allergic to my hands.
And many things that I've been given,
are hard to stomach as I smile.
So don't come around here digging,
or you will find only bones.
Where the worms who feed on my
concerns, can finally make
their thrones.

Clyde Hurlston
Of Mice & Men

Tell me that your calculations are correct,
and I can return to my normal state.
Tell me that you've gathered everything
you need, and I no longer have to wait.
Tell me that it's gone according to plan,
despite your few mistakes. Tell me certain
angles are only seen, when the body bends
before it breaks. Tell me anything with
certainty, and I'll believe every letter of
the lie. Then tell me this latest twist was
just a part, of a new hypothesis to try.
For I've grown tired of every poke and prod,
So won't you bring this study to an end?
Make brimstone rain down upon us all,
the way that you did back then.
Or do you find joy within the suffering,
of we mice inside the maze?
Parameters set, you let us loose,
to go round in circles through the days.
Do you acknowledge follies when they rear,
their ugly heads to be seen?
Or do you blame the lowly mouse,
for not adhering to scripts inside your
dream? Well stop the ride, I'm getting off,
I'd rather live my days alone.
For there is no cheese beyond the veil,
that's what this experiment has shown.
So leave the insignificant to their own device,
with only will to be their guide.
For the best laid plans of mice and men,
often result in deaths or tainted pride.

A DEBT PAID IN INK

This Brand Of Execution

They say I waste too many days, wrapped up in my head. And I waste too many nights, just lying in the bed. When I should be living out, the dreams I used to dream. 'Cause now I walk outside, and it makes me want to scream. And I know these words may sound, like things I've said before. But you should know the difference is, this time I mean it more. So please believe me when I say... This brand of execution, is better for results. 'Cause now I feel alive, so stop checking for my pulse. And strap in for a ride, as I aim for the sky. 'Cause the life I was denied, will be mine before I die. And I've wasted every chance, to tell you how I feel. 'Cause my heart's a gaping wound, that just won't seem to heal. But I should never fault you, for things you didn't do. And just commend the rougher seas, that you've ridden through. And I know these words may sound, like things I've said before. But you should know the difference is, this time I mean it more. So please believe me when I say... This brand of execution, is better for results. 'Cause now I feel alive, so stop checking for my pulse. And strap in for a ride, as I aim for the sky. 'Cause the life I was denied, will be mine before I die. See, I was once the portrait, a life of wasted paint. And I never gave solutions, just tired, old complaints. So it made people disappear, and, I then grew into this. Through fault that was my own, there was so much that I missed. And I'm too far from perfect, to ever get it back. But I acknowledge all the things, I'm feeling that I lack. But now I need room, to try and spread the wings. That often weighed me down, now they'll get me off the ground. And I know these words may sound, like things I've said before. But you should know the difference is, this time I mean it more. So please believe me when I say... This brand of execution, is better for results. 'Cause now I feel alive, so stop checking for my pulse. And strap in for a ride, as I aim for the sky. 'Cause the life I was denied, will be mine before I die. And I've found there's beauty in the darkness, and there's ugliness in light. I'm so tired of wasting, both the day and the night. And I'll close my eyes, because I just want to breathe. The taste of the air, that once caused me to seethe. Because it was filled, with the smell of a life. That I was too scared to live, so now, I close my eyes and say. This brand of execution, is better for results. 'Cause now I feel alive, so stop checking for my pulse. And strap in for a ride, as I aim for the sky. 'Cause the life I was denied, will be mine before I die. And I know these words may sound, like things I've said before. But you should know the difference is, this time I mean it more. And I know my promises were like, fingernails I used to bite. 'Cause I never noticed them, until they came undone. But to the people that I've hurt, or the ones still throwing dirt. You will see me smile and say, look at all that I've become. And whether it's for better or for worse, I had to get started moving first. Instead of standing still, with all this time to kill. As it was pouring down the glass, into the half we'd label past. But since I can't stop the sand, I'll just have to finally take a stand. And use this brand of execution, that's better for results. 'Cause now I feel alive, so stop checking for my pulse. And strap in for a ride, since I am aiming for the sky. 'Cause the life I was denied, must be mine before I die. Yeah, it must be mine before I die, so I'm aiming for the sky. And I see I'll never reach it, if I don't get off my ass and try. To shake the disposition, that's felt so much like home. And left me as the kind of man, that spends his nights alone. Because I know there's more to me, than I ever tried to see. And I'm more than capable, of being the man I'd like to be. So get started making way, I'll greet no obstacle today. And according to my pulse, I'll have plenty more to say. And I know these words may sound, like things I've said before. But you should know the difference is, this time I mean it more. So will you believe it this time? Or will you forget everything I've said?

CLYDE HURLSTON

Torture Through A Prism

This life is but a prism, through which you've truly shined. But to witness this is torture, or some I've come to find. For the colors you'd emit, are so very bright to see. That the morning sun is jealous, and leaves only night for me. And with no stars to decorate the darkness, I'm left to find a different source of light. So this fool will venture out alone, with such a potent urge to fight. But as all of this occurs, you're busy shining in your place. And never notice that you eclipse, the other women in your space. But like the moth closest to the flame, I will often fail to learn. That when your light is magnified, I am often left to burn. And as the smoke begins to rise, like a certain part of me. I know what'll catch your eyes, won't be hard to see. For this life is but a prism, through which you did reflect. With mosaics often made, with each glimpse we did collect. But every fleeting second, was far too short a time. So now I'm left to reckon, just how to make you mine. 'Cause I've longed to press you to the wall, like you were a poster for a child. While tearing through your clothing, like some kind of creature wild. Then I'd entice you with the whispers, of things you've seldom ever heard. Before I'd press your lips to mine, as if trying to drink your every word. But as all these thoughts occur, you're busy shining in your place. And never notice you eclipse, the other women in your space. But like the moth closest to the flame, I will often fail to learn. That when your light is magnified, I am often left to burn. And as the smoke begins to rise, like a certain part of me. I know what'll catch your eyes, won't be hard to see. Oh, this life is but a prism, that I have tried to solve. Like the cube you give to children, with the sides that do revolve. But it's a toy that's too complex, for those with a shorter fuse. See, dear, it's much like you, when you flirt and then refuse. And then you give a list of wants, that you often file as needs. While the ground that's in between us, gets overrun by weeds. But I know there have been fools, that would lie and sing your praise. And with so many blowing smoke, you got so caught up in haze. But I'm here to clear the air, using words you know are true. And darling, please believe, talking's not all this tongue can do. So if you would lay down, and put your fears to rest. I'd slowly dip below your waist, and disappear beneath your dress. Then you could use your hands, to journey through my hair. And direct my best intentions, to a place beyond compare. Until you reached the heights, that helped you talk to god. Or at least call him by his name, and know I was to blame. And yet, I'd gladly take the time, to re-trace the steps I took. If that was your current wish, that you suggested with a look. Or if you preferred another act, you'd only need to speak aloud. And I will change your body's shape, and leave you floating on a cloud. But as all these thoughts occur, you're busy shining in your place. And never notice you eclipse, the other women in your space. But like the moth closest to the flame, I will often fail to learn. That when your light is magnified, I am often left to burn. And as the smoke begins to rise, like a certain part of me. I know what'll catch your eyes, won't be hard to see. But the only question is, would you give me a chance to prove. That what I will bring to you is bliss, as you feel your body move. Or will you continue to torture me, making sure I look and never touch. Like you're excited by the fact, I've continued wanting you as much. As I have ever wanted anything, inside this life of mine. 'Cause it's hard to stop and smell the roses, when you're viewed solely as a vine...

What A World

It breaks my heart to see this world as it is.
I take a look around, and I see serpents slither
proudly, trying to wind their way into office.
I see true salesmen, offering the deal of an
after-lifetime, while standing at the pulpits.
Ready to euthanize free thoughts,
with their certainty wrapped in bravado.
I see heroes afraid to stand, or in some cases
take a knee; because they usually have to
stand alone. I see the massive flock of sheep,
that will turn to hornets when they're
offended. Back home, I see kings and
queens, behaving like they're jesters and
peasants. And sadly, I've even seen an
angel kept under glass.
Trapped like a butterfly.
Held in place by sharp objects behind
her eyes. What a world this is.
Ugliness and selfishness are promoted.
While grace and magnificence are ignored.
Even by those who possess them.
And to think, they actually swear and
believe, their shepherd is in a rush to
come back to this place.

CLYDE HURLSTON

Burn Brightly

Life is funny sometimes…
Equal parts kind and cruel.
Displaying both beauty and horror.
Often showing us the depths in
our heights. And their counterparts
for good measure. Yet, my point in
all of this, is that we must fight.
Fight until our last breaths are
softly exhaled. Fight until our death
throes fall prey to rigor mortis.
Fight until our accomplishments,
Take the shape of memories.
Friend, we must fight to keep our
flames alight. And bid them to burn
brightly, like the pyres of lore.
For we'll always be at the mercy of
the wind. But we must not let time
extinguish our resolve.
Nor should it succeed in
smothering our passions.
Not while there are so many
things we've yet to taste.
So many tasks left undone,
So many stones unturned.
And in all my years, I've learned…
Despite my shelf life, I am only
just getting started.

Breathe Smoke

I've endured enough in life. Having reached
both my limit and my fill. I have developed
a low tolerance for bullshit. And though, I
cannot stop the storms of life, from besieging
my patience; I will however, stop the common
from counting me amongst their ranks. I am
above their petty judgments, And
beyond their antiquated superstitions.
No, they won't stain my modernity,
With their expired trains of thought.
I am tailor made for this new age.
No longer will I give chase to those who
waste my time. Nor will I continue
extending my hand, To those too blind
to see it. I am far too tired, To convince
any of you of my worthiness.
I am worth all this world has to offer.
So decide now where you fucking stand.
And don't be surprised,
If you're left knee deep in the ashes
Of your own unreasonable expectations.
For I am no longer lost in the haze.
Now? I simply breathe smoke.

Pyrrhic Victory

Le mie parole sono le mie armi.
Con loro, io sono invincibile.

Words written in tongues my own
cannot speak, doesn't make them
any less true. My gift is my curse,
and so I mine the best from my worst.
And I am slowly learning who I am today.
And I am truly grateful.
For the fool I was then,
has now grown wiser from defeat.
And even Pyrrhic victories can be sweet.
For I will not let the bitterness consume
me any longer. I rest knowing that life is
the fire we are forged in, And the flames
have made me stronger. So now, I don't
bend, my friend. I endure.

Red Flags

There are dark days ahead.
It's not safe anymore.
So I guess it's time we armed
ourselves. Not necessarily with
guns, but rather with experience.
And eyes trained, to red flags
anywhere besides hindsight.
Because in truth, people often
show you who they really are.
But there's something within us,
that makes us ignore the signs.
And so, we focus only on the smiles.
Usually failing to realize,
that those are awfully, big teeth
they have. I guess the flashing box
cries wolf too often. So nobody
believes the patterns,
until it is far too late.

Mosaics

So many people are broken. And in my heart, I sympathize with them. For I know the depths of the personal abyss. But honestly, I'm just tired. So I no longer have the patience, To put people back together again. Especially when they keep running back, to the places where they were shattered. I want to be sorry, but I'm not. I've lost my love for making mosaics. The rewards don't justify the effort.

The Depths

Good ideas will spark inspiration. While poor ideas, they will spark condemnation. But when at the mercy of the moment, you're not sure which is which. That is why you must take the proverbial leap.
You only know the depths of the waters, after you've properly tested them. And how ironic is it, that when you push past boundaries in the world, what you truly do
is open them within yourself.

CLYDE HURLSTON

Mistress

Life is a strange mistress.
Often brutal, uncompromising.
Other times she's gentle, even loving.
Her love is equal parts sunshine and storms.
And I wouldn't trade her for the world.

A DEBT PAID IN INK

This book that you have just read was the culmination of years of my life. Writing has truly been the one thing that has saved me. This is my therapy. Within this book, you have witnessed my heart and my soul, my sweat and my tears. I am both humbled and grateful that you have chosen to take the time to read these words. But now that you have, I must take the time and pay my respects to those who have supported me. Thank you all so very much for helping me to make my dreams come true. May this be the inspiration you need, to pursue your own. I love you all.

This collection of poetry is dedicated with love to the memory of Shawn E. Ebanks.
I carry you with me always.

www.ingramcontent.com/pod-product-compliance
Lightning Source LLC
Chambersburg PA
CBHW051843160426
43209CB00006B/1132